DISTRIBUTIVE JUSTICE

A Constructive Critique of the
Utilitarian Theory of Distribution

DISTRIBUTIVE JUSTICE

Nicholas Rescher
University Professor of Philosophy
University of Pittsburgh

UNIVERSITY
PRESS OF
AMERICA

University Press of America, Inc.™
P.O. Box 19101, Washington, D.C. 20036

Printed in the United States of America

ISBN   (Perfect): 0-8191-2686-1

Library of Congress Number: 82-45162

For
WILFRID SELLARS
Colleague and Friend

Ac primum in hoc Panaetius defendendus est, quod non utilia cum honestis pugnare aliquando posse dixerit (neque enim ei fas erat), sed ea, quae viderentur utilia. Nihil vero utile, quod non idem honestum, nihil honestum, quod non idem utile sit, saepe testatur negatque ullam pestem maiorem in vitam hominum invasisse quam eorum opinonem, qui ista distraxerint. Itaque, non ut aliquando anteponeremus utilia honestis, sed ut ea sine errore diiudicaremus, si quando incidissent, induxit eam, quae videretur esse, non quae esset, repugnantiam.

In the first place, we must defend Panaetius on this point; for he has said, not that the truly utile could at times clash with the just—for he could not legitimately have said that—but only that what *seemed* utile could do so. For he often bears witness to the fact that nothing is *genuinely* utile that is not at the same time just, and nothing just that is not at the same time utile; and he holds that no greater curse has ever assailed human life than the doctrine of those who have separated these two. And so he held, not that the utile sometimes be given preference over the just, but that in cases when they [apparently] clash, we might decide between them without uncertainty, because they merely seem opposed but are not actually so.

Cicero, De officiis III. 7.

PREFACE

A book on the topic of "distributive justice" might plausibly be expected to be a work of passion: the issue is one of those high-energy fuels of controversy capable of generating a great deal of heat. One way of looking at the problem is from the perspective of the discontented poor man, wroth at the disparity between himself and the rich, and yearning on grounds of "justice" for egalitarian rectification. Another perspective is that of the uneasily contented rich man who, ill at ease about this same disparity, is eager to defend on systematic grounds the "justice" of the social arrangements which permit and perpetuate it. The topic is one that virtually demands a polemical tract. However, the reader who expects to meet one in the present work will have his expectations disappointed. This book addresses itself not so much to the large fabric of the ethical theory of social polity, as to the smaller, largely conceptual issues that lurk within the grand theories as threads holding the parts together. Saying this is not, however, as modest as it sounds. Our smaller considerations are not irrelevant to the larger doctrines: where the threads are poor, the whole garment comes apart at the seams. At any rate we are here not engaged upon the partisan work of the social critic or apologist, but the impartial work of the philosopher—to elicit the implications inherent in key concepts, to draw essential distinctions, to note inescapable difficulties, to insist upon considerations that must be taken into account. If our deliberations lead to any upshot of a doctrinal character, it is this: the issues are so complex and ramified that any simplicistic doctrine proposing an easy answer to the riddle of distributive justice can be dismissed out of hand.

It may help the reader to orient himself if I acknowledge my indebtedness to two previous writings, *The Methods of Ethics* by the subtle and profound utilitarian Henry Sidgwick, and *The Right and the Good* by the sagacious antiutilitarian W. D. Ross. These writers seem to me to lay the groundwork for the position I myself find congenial: a chastened utilitarianism, purged of exclusivity claims, and prepared to acknowledge the need for according to principles distinct from the principle of utility—preeminently that of justice—a place coequal with, rather than subordinate to, the utilitarian principle.

In writing the book I have profited greatly from discussions with three colleagues at the University of Pittsburgh: Kurt Baier, Nuel D. Belnap, Jr., and David Braybrooke. My colleague Jerome Schneewind made valuable suggestions regarding the Bibliography. I am grateful for the assistance that several graduate students rendered in a variety of ways, ranging from manuscript criticism to help in preparing the Bibliography and in proofreading. The recording of their names is an obligation whose discharge gives me much pleasure: Bliss Cartwright, Douglas E. Hosler, Anne Hunt, Stephen Norris, Michael Pelon, and Souren Teghrarian. Professors A. G. N. Flew of the University of Keele and J. J. C. Smart of the University of Adelaide were kind enough to read the material in draft form, affording me the opportunity to benefit by their comments and criticisms. Last though not least I am indebted to Miss Dorothy Henle and Mrs. Arthur C. Laubach for transforming my hen scratches into a typescript acceptable to the printer, and to Miss Henle for helping me to see the work through the press.

The writing of this book constituted a part of my contribution to an investigation of values in general, and current American values in particular, conducted at the University of Pittsburgh with the support of grants from the Carnegie Corporation of New York and the International Business Machines Corporation. It is a matter of great pleasure to me to record grateful thanks for this support.

NICHOLAS RESCHER

Pittsburgh
July 1965

CONTENTS

xiii

3. Legitimate Claims

4. The Canons of Distributive Justice and the Foundations of Claims

5. Complications Affecting the Justice of Distributions

6. *The Proper Sphere of the Principle of Utility*

Bibliography

Indexes

DISTRIBUTIVE JUSTICE

A Constructive Critique of the
Utilitarian Theory of Distribution

1

---

*The Problem
of
Distributive
Justice*

---

1. Justice and Distributive Justice

Social justice is among Western man's most prized ideals and most highly treasured values. It has both a political and an economic dimension, and it is this latter, essentially economic aspect that shall concern us here. For we conceive of distributive justice as embracing the whole economic dimension of social justice, the entire question of the proper distribution of goods and services within the society.

Aristotle distinguished between a wider (universal) and a narrower (particular) sense of "justice." [1] In the wider sense, the just is *the lawful,* and justice is action in accordance with the requirements of "the law" (including the moral law as well as proper positive human law). In the narrower sense, the just is *the fair,* and justice is action in consonance with the proper interests of one's fellows, paying due regard to their honor, property, and safety. Aristotle divides justice construed in the narrower sense into two kinds:

  1) *Distributive justice,* which "is exercised in the distribution of [public assets such as] honor, wealth, and the other divisible assets of the community"; and

  2) *Corrective justice,* which "supplies a corrective principle in private transactions."

---

[1] *Nicomachean Ethics* V. 1–7. On Aristotle's theory of justice generally, see W. D. Ross, *Aristotle* (5th edn., London: Methuen & Co., 1949), ch. 7.

The main difference here seems to lie in the agent, i.e., the individual or the state; for the requirement put upon the agent, namely, that he act fairly or equitably, is clearly the same in both cases. Aristotle's *distributive justice* requires the state to act equitably in its distribution of goods (and presumably also of evils) among its members. Aristotle's *corrective justice* requires the individual to act equitably in actions or transactions affecting the interests of his fellows.

The conception of distributive justice that we shall adopt for our own purposes will be somewhat wider than Aristotle's, including a part of what he calls corrective justice. The scope of our concept will include the distribution of goods and evils generally, without regard to whether the distributing agent is an individual or person proper, or a collective individual or "person" such as a corporation or state.

Cicero, and the Roman jurists generally, adopted the dictum that justice consists in "giving to each his own" (*suum cuique tribuens*).[2] This is a matter of relatively little difficulty when the distribution at issue is one of giving back to the individual something he already owns. But when a distribution of as yet unowned goods is in question, the individual by hypothesis *owns* nothing; at the most, the thing he "has" is *a claim* (or perhaps *an obligation,* when an evil rather than a good is being distributed). Here, then, justice consists in realizing to the greatest possible extent a distribution that renders to each a "fair share" of the good (or evil) at issue.

It is not surprising that we owe to the Romans some of the most acute insights into the nature of justice: justice is among the more legalistic of ethical concepts. For this very reason it is not the ultimate factor in ethics. A juster world is not necessarily a morally superior one: in an emphasis upon justice there is a somewhat carping insistence upon giving and getting "one's due share" that ignores the dimension of generosity, sacrifice, self-abnegation, and deeds of supererogation.

[2] Jesus' advice to "Render unto Caesar that which is Caesar's and unto God that which is God's" is a strict parallel.

From an ethical standpoint, the Dispensation of Justice has something of the Old Testament air of an insistence upon the bare minimalities. The result is that writers on ethics traditionally contrast *justice* with *benevolence,* recognizing that the line of division is not perfectly sharp, because, as Sidgwick put it, there is a "borderland, tenanted with expectations which are not quite claims and with regard to which we do not feel sure whether Justice does or does not require us to satisfy them." [8]

2. The Task of a Theory of Distributive Justice

The task of a theory of distributive justice is to provide the machinery in terms of which one can assess the relative merits or demerits of a distribution, the "assessment" in question being made from the moral or ethical point of view. Its objective is to establish a *principle* by which the "assessment" of alternative possible distributions can be carried out.

It is clearly not sufficient that a principle of distributive justice should tell us only about the ideal distribution, the very best of possible alternatives. For to apply any such principle in practice we must know which of several feasible nonideal alternatives is to be preferred: we must know not only what is *the best,* but must be able to determine—in the great majority of cases, at any rate—which of several alternative possibilities is "the better." A principle of evaluation is not adequate if it merely depicts a theoretical ideal that we cannot apply in practice to determine which of several putative possibilities comes "closer to the ideal." (How far has the beginner come toward learning how to evaluate bridge hands when he is told that the ideal holding consists of the four aces, the four kings, the four queens, and a jack?)

What is needed is something to which writers on ethics—

[8] Henry Sidgwick, *The Methods of Ethics* (7th edn., London: Macmillan, 1907), p. 270.

and, for that matter, writers on economics also—have been loath to address themselves, *a criterion of merit for suboptimal alternatives*. The evaluation criterion of an adequate theory of distributive justice must be capable not simply of absolute *idealization* (i.e., of telling us what the ideal is), but also of relative *evaluation* (i.e., of telling us which of several possible alternatives is to be regarded as the most satisfactory).

Distributive justice—exactly like punitive justice—can be brought to realization only in *this* world, that is, in an imperfect world populated by imperfect men. A perfectly just system of punitive justice would apprehend, process, and punish all and only the guilty, and would ignore, leave unprocessed and unpunished, all and only the innocent. But any realizable system will be such that it cannot fail to depart from the ideal in several ways (say, by catching some of the innocent and by letting escape some of the guilty). And these modes of injustice are interrelated and interlocked: as we modify the system to avoid injustices of the one kind, we *ipso facto* increase those of another. In evaluating alternative procedures in criminal law and law enforcement we have to be prepared to make choices among the realizable, and thus less-than-ideal, alternatives; exactly the same is true in evaluating socio-economic arrangements with respect to their accordance or violation with the principles of distributive justice.

3. *The Principle of Utility*

We shall base our inquiry into the principle of distributive justice upon an investigation of the doctrine of utilitarianism. This doctrine is founded upon the *principle of utility*, which asserts that utility (or, if you wish, simply the good things of this life) should be distributed according to the rule of "the greatest good of the greatest number." Exact as it sounds, this classic principle is imprecise and indeed inadequate. The first objective of our discussion is to exhibit these shortcomings in considerable detail. And when the necessary emendations are made, the resulting position will be such that the label "utilitarian" (as usually construed) can be pinned to it only with serious reservations and qualifications, if at all. We shall use this critique of the principle of utility to illustrate the very complex and inherently problematic character of the concept of distributive justice.

Some of the classical utilitarians have taken the principle of utility to relate to human actions in general, and not to be confined specifically to distributions of goods. Insofar as the majority of human actions have consequences affecting others favorably or unfavorably, they "distribute" utilities (or disutilities) to the parties concerned. So regarded, all actions affecting others become "distributions of utilities," and the principle of utility can be applied, thus widening its scope from that of a mere principle of distributive justice to a general criterion of right action in human conduct. For the present, however, we must take a limited view of the principle of utility, without reference to its oft maintained role as a criterion of right action in human conduct. We shall resist—at any rate for the time being—this expansion of its scope, confining its application to genuine distributions. But at a later stage of the inquiry we shall return to the conception of the principle of utility as a general arbiter in ethics.

4. The Problem of the Viability of the Utility Concept

At the outset we face the objection that when we talk of dividing *utility* we actually do not know what we are talking about. Just what exactly is "utility"? Is not utility a treacherous abstraction beguiling us into a misleading monistic simplification, whereas in reality there is at issue an enormous plurality of goods and value-measures of very different kinds? Let this admitted difficulty not hobble our enterprise at the very outset. Let us simply gloss "utility" as the sum total of "the good things of life," also making due allowance for the evils. (Presumably the avoidance of suffering is a more significant element of "utility" than the promotion of happiness.[4])

Although nineteenth-century Anglo-American economics relied heavily upon the conception of utility (provoking Karl Nietzsche to the extent of remarking that "Man does not desire happiness, only an Englishman does!"), the welfare economists ultimately became disillusioned with it. They ran into a quagmire of difficulty in doing what for their purposes was essential: providing a means for the actual measurement of utility, the specific determination of utility values. The difficulties lay in the move from the valuations and preferences of individuals to an interpersonal, public measure of an intersubjective quantity of "utility." As a result, economics abandoned utility as a working instrument, and those economists who worked in a tradition most heavily reliant upon this concept, namely, the new welfare economists, shifted to lines of approach (of a nature to be discussed below) which permitted them to work in terms of subjective preferences instead of objective utilities.

The point of the concept of *utility* is to quantify diverse sorts of personal happiness and suffering for a person-to-person comparison in just the way that *monetary worth* quantifies the diverse sorts of personal property of an individual. If this conception embodies an element of blatant fiction—and it surely does so—the fiction at issue is at any rate a useful one. Let the utilitarian be given all possible benefit of doubt here. For many or most of the puzzles that arise here will also con-

---

[4] Hedonistic utilitarians have not always taken this difference into due account, a point well made by W. D. Ross, *Foundations of Ethics* (London: Oxford University Press, 1939), p. 75. Compare K. Popper on "negative utilitarianism" in *The Open Society and Its Enemies*, Vol. I (London: Routledge & Kegan Paul, 1945), ch. 9, note 2, pp. 284–285.

front us, *mutatis mutandis,* when we consider the question of
the characteristics of a just and equitable distribution of some
perfectly unproblematic good (say, money or fruitcakes),
rather than "utility." [5] All of the considerations we shall
adduce and the conclusions we shall reach—for example, that
the standards for assessing the justice of distributions vary
with circumstances, differing, say, between normal circumstances and conditions of scarcity—are fundamentally un-
changed when the distribution involves not utility, but common, garden-variety goods. The advantage of the utilitarian
approach is that it lays the groundwork for introducing into
the discussion mathematical and quantitative modes of
thought, greatly to the benefit of the exactness and clarity of
the reasoning we can bring to bear on the issues.

5. *The Influence of Utilitarianism*

The doctrine of utilitarianism has had a long and distinguished history in the course of which it has played a significant variety of roles. In the thought of Jeremy Bentham, utilitarianism was primarily a political doctrine, a guide to social
polity in the revision of existing institutions. His followers
(from Mill to G. E. Moore) transformed it step-by-step from the
sphere of political economy to that of general ethics, leaving a
philosophical doctrine which is still very much alive and stir-
ring today—as may be seen from the Bibliography appended
to this book. Nineteenth-century economists (culminating in
Pareto) developed the doctrine on the strictly economic side,

[5] The problem we avoid with utility is that orthodox goods possess a de-
clining marginal value or "utility" (think of the traditional arguments to
justify a graduated income tax on grounds of the decreasing marginal
utility of money), although this problem could also be sidestepped by as-
suming that the discussion relates to a region where the marginal value
of the good at issue is linear (incrementally constant). For a recent attempt to put the concept of utility upon a secure conceptual basis, see
Nicholas Rescher, "Notes on Preference, Utility, and Cost," *Synthèse,*
XIX (1967).

and it became the foundation of the welfare economics of the twentieth century. Gradually penetrating beyond the restrictive confines of any technical discipline—a process aided by such politico-economic movements as the Fabian Society—utilitarianism has today made its way deep into the popular folklore of democratic theorizing *via* its entry into such (otherwise far older) concepts as "the common good" and "the public interest." A. D. Lindsay aptly spoke of the utilitarians as "that remarkable school of thinkers and writers who left their mark so deep on nineteenth-century England, whose influence still works powerfully in us even when we least recognize it." [6]

With such widespread diffusion of the influence of the utilitarian principle, "the greatest good of the greatest number," clearly import of a more than narrow and technically philosophical kind attaches to a demonstration of its loose, foggy, and genuinely problematic character.

6. *Distributive Justice and the Welfare Economists*

Although modern welfare economics has, as we have seen, effectively given up the conception of an interpersonal utility, it has introduced various substitutes which render its deliberations still germane to our topic. The starting point here is the now classic strategem of Vilfredo Pareto.[7] According to Pareto,

---

[6] Preface to the English translation by Mary Morris, of E. Halévy, *The Growth of Philosophic Radicalism* (London: Faber & Gwyer, 1928). And as B. de Jouvenel put it, "In fact the mode of thought which tends to predominate in advanced circles is nothing but the tail-end of nineteenth-century utilitarianism" (*The Ethics of Redistribution* [Cambridge: Cambridge University Press, 1951], p. 48).

[7] *Manuel d'économie politique*, trans. A. Bonnet (Paris: V. Giard & E. Brière, 1909; 2nd edn., Paris, 1927). Cf. the account of Pareto's views in T. W. Hutchinson, *A Review of Economic Doctrines, 1870–1929* (Oxford: The Clarendon Press, 1953). Note that the position advanced in the quotation, in taking the standpoint of searching for all-benefiting improvements upon a fixed initial position, ignores whatever shortcomings that

the utilitarian's problem of "obtaining the maximum of well-being for a collectivity" may be settled if we:

> consider any particular position and suppose that a very small move is made [from it] . . . [Then if] the well-being of all the individuals is increased, it is evident that the new position is more advantageous for each one of them; vice versa it is less so if the well-being of all the individuals is diminished. The well-being of some may remain the same without these conclusions being affected. But if, on the other hand, the small move increases the well-being of certain individuals, and diminishes that of others, it can no longer be said that it is advantageous to the community as a whole to make such a move.[8]

This conception of the matter leads to the idea of a *Pareto improvement* upon an initial distribution as any alternative distribution according to which every participant fares no worse than (i.e., fares better or as well as) he does on the initial distribution. We arrive also at the idea of a *Pareto optimal* distribution within a set of alternatives as any distribution within the set that is such that none of the other distributions in the set effect a Pareto improvement upon it. In the determination of such an improvement or optimum we need not make any interpersonal comparisons at all. This consideration was viewed by Pareto as having crucial programmatic significance. For on his view of the matter, the only welfare or well-being that comes within the purview of economics is simply what the individual himself judges to be his well-being, his *subjective* utility, or "ophelimity," as Pareto himself called it.

There are several serious difficulties with Pareto's approach. In the first place, many real-life cases set before us situations in which no available alternative distribution is a Pareto improvement, all of them requiring that some persons (however

initial position may have—from the standpoint of distributive justice, for example.

[8] *Ibid.*, pp. 617–618; tr. in Hutchinson, p. 225.

few) must yield something (however little) for the advantage of the rest. At the other extreme, problems arise when there are several alternative Pareto improvements. When best comes to best, one of these may prove to be such that it *dominates* all its alternatives in the sense that according to it, *every* participant fares no worse than (i.e., fares better or as well as) he fares on any of the others. But to look for such dominating solutions in practical economies is, for the most part, to look for the pot of gold at the end of the rainbow: usually there is an embarrassment of riches as regards diverse Pareto optima. And the shortcoming of the Pareto approach is the unresolved state in which it leaves the problem of preferential choice among suboptimal alternatives. Not only does Pareto's comparison-avoidance policy not resolve this problem, it provides a rationale within which it is "bad form" even to ask for guidance toward a solution.

Nor has this situation been improved upon in the "New Welfare Economics." The manifesto of this school was issued in Nicholas Kaldor's important paper of 1939.[9] The question of the distribution of income, Kaldor argued, is an ethical question, which economists would do well to sidestep entirely, since it is "quite impossible to decide on economic grounds what particular pattern of income-distribution maximizes social welfare." [10] Kaldor in effect urged a separation between questions of production on the one hand and questions of distribution on the other, holding that the economist should concentrate his efforts upon the former and let others (presumably the politicians) worry about the second. He maintained that:

> In all cases . . . where a certain policy leads to an increase in physical productivity, and thus of aggregate real income, the economist's case for the policy is quite unaffected by the ques-

[9] "Welfare Propositions in Economics and Interpersonal Comparisons of Utility," *Economic Journal*, XLIX (1939), 549–552.
[10] *Ibid.*, p. 549.

tion of the comparability of individual satisfactions; since in all such cases it is *possible* to make everybody better off than before, or at any rate to make some people better off without making anybody worse off. There is no need for the economist to prove —as indeed he never could prove—that as a result of the adoption of a certain measure nobody in the community is going to suffer. In order to establish his case, it is quite sufficient for him to show that even if all those who suffer as a result are fully compensated for their loss, the rest of the community will still be better off than before. Whether the landlords, in the free-trade case, should in fact be given compensation or not is a political question on which the economist, *qua* economist, could hardly pronounce an opinion.[11]

Kaldor supported his thesis, that economists should concern themselves with increasing production without worrying about distribution of the resultant income, by the very interesting line of reasoning that when the total amount of new goods and services is increased, then the result is to be regarded as superior from the economists' point of view, because it is *in principle possible* for the beneficiaries of the augmented situation to induce the losers to accept it by compensating (or even overcompensating, i.e., rewarding) them for adopting the new scheme rather than continuing with the old. In the wake of J. R. Hicks's endorsement of Kaldor's conceptions in an influential article,[12] "The Kaldor Compensation Principle" has also become known as "The Kaldor-Hicks Criterion."

That this principle or criterion rests, as far as actual economic practice is concerned, upon simple outright mythology is perfectly evident. There is no reason in theory, and little evidence in practice, to think that the beneficiaries of a new economic arrangement are likely to compensate those who sustain losses thereby. Rosy opportunities for general improvements often turn, in the cooler light of morning, to grey actu-

11 *Ibid.*
12 J. R. Hicks, "The Foundations of Welfare Economics," *Economic Journal*, XLIX (1939), 696–712.

alities that advance special interests, doing so in ways that could and should have been foreseen. If one is going to motivate economic measures in terms of a social-contract-for-the-general-advantage conception, one must undertake a responsibility to assure in advance that the terms of this contract are reasonably realistic ones.

Moreover, and even more seriously, in addition to its reliance on the mythology of compensatory redistribution, the Kaldor-Hicks criterion rests on an abstraction the acceptance of which does serious damage to our understanding of the economic facts: the conception that production and distribution may be treated as *independent* variables, so that any mode of distribution of a product is in practice economically compatible with a given set of arrangements for its production. To think of the product of an ongoing economy as redistributable at will is to abstract from the fact that an economy is a complex network of institutions, practices, and arrangements which limit the possibilities of distribution in various, and sometimes very drastic respects. What we confront is an economic *system* of such a kind that the way in which a productive sector is organized is so bound up with the question of distribution that it creates a set of claims on the product, claims which cannot be violated systematically. And should the machinery of distribution be revised to run counter to those claims, a breakdown or malfunction of the productive functioning of the system would result. In a going economy, then, production and distribution are not independent variables: rather, they are so interrelated that one cannot be varied without the other. We must not think, even in the first approximation, that the goods and services representing a product of an economy represent a stockpile that one is free to distribute or redistribute at will.

Let us turn for a moment from the question of the *correctness* of the Kaldor-Hicks criterion to that of its *function*. What it does is to serve as a smokescreen, hiding unconcern with a certain set of problems, and as an excuse for passing these unwanted problems on to somebody else. The position espoused by these economic authorities may be put something like this: "We economists, as social scientists, describe and do not evaluate; we provide expert technical guidance on means, and do not issue prescriptions as to ends. The only normative judgment we are prepared to underwrite is the virtually descriptive platitude that the function of an economic system is the production of goods and services.[13] Very well, then, let us economists study how this production can be augmented. The normative problem of how this added product should be distributed is no doubt a real problem, but (except perhaps insofar as maldistribution may hinder production) it is not *our* problem—it is a problem for the politicians and the political process." The tendency of the welfare economists is simply to divest economics of concern with the very problem we set ourselves here—that of evaluating distributions. Apart from a dutiful, polite bow in the direction of egalitarianism,[14] modern Anglo-American economics has tended to refuse to confront our problem on the relevant terms, and thus provides little guidance toward its solution.

In saying this we do not mean to reproach the economists for making increased production the first order of business, tabling the issue of distribution for future consideration. There is, as we shall see in Chapter Five below, substantial justification—even from the standpoint of distributive justice —for putting considerations of production ahead of those of distribution under certain circumstances. The step the wel-

---

[13] For an eloquent and influential statement of this point of view, see L. Robbins, *An Essay on the Nature and Significance of Economic Science* (London: Macmillan, 1932).

[14] This perhaps puts the matter somewhat—but only a little—too strongly. A notable exception is A. C. Pigou's *The Economics of Welfare* (London, 1920; 4th edn., 1932), which presents an eloquent and reasoned defense of economic egalitarianism.

fare economists have taken in putting questions of distribution aside may well be defensible. But to say this is certainly not to deny that the reasons advanced for taking this step are in some ways little better than myths.[15]

7. *Methodological Preliminaries*

The methodology to be employed in the examination of principles of distributive justice is very simple. It is that of *confronting the principle with hypothetical examples of a choice between specified alternative distributions of a certain putative good among certain recipients.* On this approach, the adequacy of a contemplated principle will be assessed in terms of its ability to answer in a *nonequivocal and not patently unacceptable* way the question of which (if any) among a given group of individuals is to be preferred. This technique of analysis places heavy reliance upon the reader's ability to make "correct" intuitive appraisals about the relative justness of alternative distributions. It smacks of a "moral sense" approach —not, to be sure, as regards an insight into principles, but as regards the appraisal of particular cases. We endorse and adopt the methodological principle put forward by W. D. Ross:

> I will maintain, in fact, that what we are apt to describe as "what we think" about moral questions . . . forms the standard reference to which the truth of any moral theory has to be tested, instead of having itself to be tested by reference to any theory.[16]

[15] In this section I have drawn heavily upon I. M. D. Little's *A Critique of Welfare Economics* (2nd edn., Oxford: The Clarendon Press, 1957), and D. Braybrooke, "Farewell to the New Welfare Economics," *The Review of Economic Studies*, XXIII (1955), 180–193.

[16] W. D. Ross, *The Right and the Good* (Oxford: The Clarendon Press, 1930), p. 40. Compare F. Y. Edgeworth's apt observation that " 'philosophical intuitionism' does not come to destroy common-sense, but to fulfil it, systematizing it and rendering it consistent with itself" (*Mathematical Psychics* [London: Kegan Paul, 1881], p. 128).

It goes perhaps without saying that the validity of this methodological principle is restricted to the testing and validation of theories regarding matters of value, and that it is inapplicable in the context of theories regarding matters of fact.

This technique of inquiry gives our discussion an underpinning of solidity and uniformity on the methodological side. The criticisms we shall deploy against the utilitarian theory are (in the main) not new, but have for the most part been made before. Here however the entire critique develops as the systematic unfolding of the consequences of a single and uniform methodological principle.

The great and immediate advantage of this approach is that it wholly avoids one of the red-herring side issues that obscures a clear analysis of the classical version of utilitarianism: the issue of consequences. Classical utilitarians would have us choose that mode of action whose (foreseeable and probable) causal consequences are such as to result in "the greatest good of the greatest number." This point of view is *prospective,* whereas ours is to be *retrospective.* In formulating our approach in terms of a direct choice among completed presumptive result-states—ultimate outcomes after everything is "said and done"—we are able to short-circuit the entire *empirical* issue of causal consequences. Moreover, we preclude the possibility of an "under-the-table" redistribution of the given division, say, by some or all of those who fare well by its adoption compensating some or all of those who do not.

An important ambiguity in talking about the "result of a distribution" must be resolved: Are we to think only of the *incremental changes* made within the distribution, or of the entire resultant position that exists after the distribution is made? In terms of an economic analogy, is the distribution at issue one of income or one of wealth? Here our standard point of view will be a somewhat artificial one: we shall conceive of distributions incrementally, but as involving increments (positive or negative) occurring around essentially the same initial position. In terms of the economic analogy, we think of distributions of income that are construed as affecting persons whose initial wealth is to be taken—in the absence of explicit assumptions to the contrary—as essentially identical in the relevant respects.

Our procedure also postulates the causal inefficacy of the persons involved in the distribution. We want to assess the merit of the distributions themselves, not the moral qualities of the persons who might put them into effect. Thus if ten units of a good are to be divided among three claimants, Messrs A, B, and C, who are to get shares (a), (b), and (c), respectively, and this is to be done by Mr. A., the intrinsically indifferent distributions

Share	SCHEME I	SCHEME II	SCHEME III
(a)	3 units	3 units	4 units
(b)	3	4	3
(c)	4	3	3

obtain an ethically diverse character by the fact of A's agency, in that, though in selecting Scheme I and Scheme II he would not be acting selfishly, in selecting Scheme III he would be. When the distributions are assumed to come about through no involvement of the participants in any way, the whole issue of self-interest, interest, and disinterest is avoided. In this way, too, we sidestep the whole issue of the *ways and means* of distribution, raising the possibility of "just distributions unjustly arrived at," and also the question of *who* is supposed to be making the choice among alternative distributions and *with what right*. (If a commissar or economic czar or confiscatory dictator is distributing national wealth, it can plausibly be argued that *the whole procedure* is unjust, regardless of how just *the distribution of goods* that he arrives at may be.) Our focus shall be exclusively upon the comparative justness of alternative distributions in themselves, waiving, insofar as possible, all such issues relating to the *context* of the distribution.

In taking this externalistic, noncausal approach we depart to some extent from the usual stance of utilitarian theorizing: looking at the resulting situation *as a whole* we take the standpoint of an external "off-stage" observer, or, if you prefer, a historical observer appraising matters from an *ex post facto* perspective. The point is that the evaluations of such an observer have no causal effects within the domain with respect to which these evaluations are made. We deliberately avoid the standpoint of an actor on the moral stage whose moral evaluations and choices will themselves have distinctive future consequences (realizing that the actions that are the immediate objects of evaluation must be viewed in the context of such "secondary effects" as the influence of the choice upon others, or upon the character of the agent). We are to make essentially retrospective judgments of preference among *wholly defined alternatives* involving human actions, together with their *specific*, determinate set of (presumptive) consequences, rather than looking upon the evaluation as a historical transaction that itself lies within the course of human events oriented toward a developing, open future.

An approach via the concept of an intersubjective utility introduces the objectivistic point of view that greatly facilitates the discussion of problems relating to distributive justice. For the type of question at issue here is typified by the choice of alternative ways of *dividing a certain (essentially homogeneous) body of goods among a group of (potential) recipients*. And we do not need, for our central purpose, to get enmeshed in the subjectivistic difficulties arising, for example, when, although *X's actual* share stands in a ratio of 4:1 to *Y*'s, the inordinately grasping *X* nevertheless *feels* that this ratio is 1:4. The main problems to be dealt with can all be raised and resolved (if at all, then) from the angle of dividing a given body of goods among recipients all of whom assess the values at issue by the same standards and on the same scale of valuation.[17]

It is inevitable that this sort of analysis must make some abstraction from the wealth of concrete detail present in actual cases. This does not constitute an insuperable roadblock, in view of the fact that our purposes are adequately served by the concept of a "prima-facie preferable distribution" wholly analogous to the concept of a "prima-facie duty" in ethical theory. To say that X has the prima-facie duty to pay Y $10 today because he borrowed the money a week ago and promised to return it today is to say that *IF all the relevant facts that have a bearing upon X's duties are as described,* (i.e., if none of the unmentioned facts constitute countervailing considerations (for example, that X has a similar debt to Z but only has a total resource of $18), THEN, under this hypothesis of "unchangeability by the unmentioned," the purported duty at issue would be his actual duty. The case is similar with the distribution we select as prima-facie preferable within the range of our abstractly characterized distribution situations. Here we make only the hypothetical contention that IF all the relevant facts that have a bearing upon the relative merits of the alternative distributions at issue are as described (i.e., if none of the unmentioned facts constitute countervailing considerations), THEN the indicated distribution at issue would be the best or most appropriate distribution.

[17] Our supposition also obviates the difficulty raised by Henry Sidgwick (*Methods of Ethics,* Book IV, ch. 1) that any actual distribution deals with the *means of happiness,* whereas the utilitarian principle concerns itself with happiness as such. It postulates the supposition that the quantity of the resultant utility (happiness) is proportional to the share of the good (means) whose distribution is at issue.

2

---

*Analysis
of the
Utilitarian
Formula*

---

1. The Principle of Utility Is a Two-Factor Criterion

Suppose that some three particular persons, Messrs *A, B,* and *C,* can be given the utility shares (a), (b), and (c), respectively, in accordance with either Scheme I or Scheme II: [1]

Share	SCHEME I	SCHEME II
(a)	3 units	2 units
(b)	3	2
(c)	3	6

Which scheme represents the superior mode of distribution? Scheme II yields "the greater good": it distributes ten units as compared with the nine of its rival. Scheme I yields a greater advantage in goods for "the greater number": two persons gain by its adoption and only one loses. The example brings out the fact that *the principle of utility is a two-factor criterion* ("greater good," "greater number"), and that these two factors can in given cases work against one another. There is thus nothing in the principle of utility itself to help us in making—let alone in dictating a particular outcome of—a

[1] We are to think of the indicated shares here *not* as representing marginal utility increments added to an otherwise fixed initial amount, but as the *total resultant* utility distribution after whatever distributing mechanism may be supposed operative has done its work.

choice between Scheme I and Scheme II. The principle unqualified is patently incomplete as an effective means for de-
ciding between alternative distributions of a good.

Some utilitarians have, at least seemingly, gone from a two-
factor to a one-factor criterion, placing their sole reliance
upon "the greater good," dropping the last four words from
the utilitarian formula. (Bentham himself inclined to this view
in his later days,[2] reasoning, along lines shortly to be described, that the greater good *requires* greater numbers.) But
despite its greater logical tidiness, the view that the eligibility
of a proposed action with its consequent distribution of utility
turns solely on the *total* good involved, without any regard
whatsoever to the *pattern of its distribution,* is pretty obviously unacceptable. On the other hand, it would obviously not
do to place, in a burst of democratic enthusiasm, an *exclusive*
reliance on "the greater number."[3] For consider the
distributions:

Share	SCHEME I	SCHEME II
(a)	5 units	4 units
(b)	5	4
(c)	5	3
(d)	1	3
(e)	1	3

Doubtless the greater number of recipients would opt for
Scheme I and would vote for its adoption as against Scheme II,
but it is doubtful (to say the least) that the first mode of
division is to be preferred. In such cases, even the most
ardent of democratic theoreticians have ever seen fit to safe-

---

[2] Compare F. Y. Edgeworth, *Mathematical Psychics,* pp. 117–118. Edgeworth
strongly endorses the alteration, remarking: "The principle of greatest
happiness may have gained its popularity, but lost its meaning, by the
addition '*of the greatest number.*'"

[3] We wholly ignore the ambiguity that is singled out by the question
"Greater number of *what?*" i.e., do we have an anthropocentric form of
utilitarianism, where only humans (perhaps better, *intelligent creatures*)
count, or a universalistic form, where other sentient beings are also
included?

guard the interests of minorities in ways that preclude an automatic adoption of schemes of type I.[4]

One traditional objection to utilitarianism articulated along these lines is presented in the choice between a less populous world with a higher per capita average utility, and a more populous world with a lower per capita average utility, say between:

SCHEME I	SCHEME II
	(f)
	(e)
(c)	(d)
(b)	(c)
(a)	(b)
	(a)

A contemplation of these alternatives should force an adherent of the principle of utility to decide whether by "the greatest good" he is to mean the greatest *total* good or the greatest good *per capita* (i.e., the greatest *average* good). That proto-utilitarian William Paley wrote:

> A larger portion of happiness is enjoyed amongst *ten* persons, possessing the means of healthy subsistence, than can be produced by five persons, under every advantage of power, affluence, and luxury. . . ; it follows, that the quantity of happiness in a given district, although it is possible it may be increased the number of inhabitants remaining the same, is chiefly and most naturally affected by alteration of the numbers: that, consequently, the decay of population is the greatest evil that a state can suffer; and the improvement of it the object which ought, in all countries, to be aimed at, in preference to every other political purpose whatsoever.[5]

4 It is important to qualify by safeguards of this sort the *census* technique by which D. Braybrooke and C. E. Lindblom seek to replace the classic utilitarian *calculus* in their recent book, *A Strategy of Decision* (New York: The Free Press of Glencoe, 1963).

5 William Paley, *The Principles of Moral and Political Philosophy* (7th edn., London: Baldwin & Co., 1790), Vol. II, Book VI, ch. 2, pp. 346–347.

Other—and nowadays surely more common—sentiments go the other way. Thus C. D. Broad writes:

> If Utilitarianism be true it would be one's duty to try to increase the numbers of a community, even though one reduced the average total happiness of the members, so long as the total happiness in the community would be in the least increased. It seems perfectly plain to me that this kind of action, so far from being a duty, would quite certainly be wrong.[6]

2. *A "Utility Floor" Is Needed*

Let us try the effect of one facile amendment of the principle of utility. One of the standard textbook objections to the principle is presented by the following variant of the previous example:

SCHEME I   SCHEME II

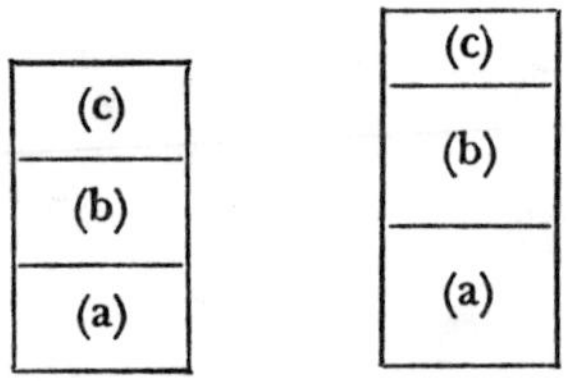

Here Scheme II not only yields "the greater good," but works to the advantage of "a greater number," since two of the three

---

Bentham, Godwin, and most early utilitarians side with Paley here. See E. Halévy, *The Growth of Philosophic Radicalism*, tr. Mary Morris, pp. 218–221. Compare also Henry Sidgwick, *The Methods of Ethics*, pp. 415–416.

[6] C. D. Broad, *Five Types of Ethical Theory* (London: Routledge & Kegan Paul, 1930), p. 250.

people involved are obvious beneficiaries of its adoption. But is it reasonable that we should in *all* such cases be prepared to sacrifice an "individual interest" in "the general benefit," as the principle of utility says we must do? The answer to this question cannot be other than *no!* We would surely not want to subject one individual to unspeakable suffering to give some insignificantly small benefit to many others (even an innumerable myriad of them).[7] Actual privation offends our sense of justice in a more serious way than do mere inequities.

These considerations suggest adding to the principle of utility another qualifying clause, a "principle of catastrophe-prevention" stipulating a minimal *utility floor* for all individuals below which no one should be pressed. The principle at issue may be regarded as being more or less built in to the very conception of a genuinely "minimally acceptable" share of good. For we would not conceive of a given level in just *this* way unless we were prepared to do battle for the rule that an exalted priority should be given to reducing to the lowest feasible number the people who receive less than this share. We might thus add to the initial principle the proviso: *provided that nobody receives less of "the good" than a certain (i.e., some plausible) minimum amount.* Clearly one of the most basic elements of our concept of justice is to minimize the number of persons in a state of genuine *deprivation* regarding their share in the available pool of utility. Diminishing the number of those who simply do not have enough is a more fundamental element of the concept of justice than diminishing the gap between the "haves" and the "have-nots."[8] And although the idea of an acceptable minimum

---

[7] A somewhat out-of-the-way example of this line of reasoning is provided by the argument of some modern theologians that creation as a whole is not worthwhile if it has the consequence of eternal damnation for some creatures.

[8] "There is a bottom level of instrumental good (money, or in this instance, food) below which equality is useless because it is equality in nothingness, or something so near to nothingness that it would be of no use to any of the recipients. No good would be achieved by requiring equality under such conditions. On the one hand, a person who

level has traditionally been stressed primarily in survival contexts, the idea has long been applied in such other connections as, for example, education.

The utilitarians of the eighteenth and early nineteenth centuries recognized and accepted this principle, and it led them to abandon, in the economic (but not the political) sphere, the egalitarianism to which they were otherwise committed:

> If the Utilitarians rejected absolute equalitarianism, it was not because they considered society as naturally hierarchical, but because they thought the quantity of subsistence actually available was not sufficient to allow all the individuals actually existing to live . . . [adequately].[9]

Apart from some such qualification, the principle of utility is clearly deficient. It is perfectly conceivable that at some historical juncture an institution of slavery, for example, could conduce to the greater good of a greater number; but we shall not be prepared to let this fact count decisively on its behalf. Again, considerations of a cognate sort led to the economic doctrine that an economy must afford every participant a "living wage." [10]

---

said, 'I know we'll all starve, but we must share equally anyway' would really be running the equality principle into the ground! Precisely the same thing has been alleged of a socialistic economy: though it provides near-equality, the incentive is so low and, human nature being what it is, the system is inevitably so inefficient that after a while there will not be much left to divide equally: we shall have what has been called a state of 'splendidly equalized destitution.' *If* it could be shown that an economy characterized by equal distribution produced this result, such an economy would be almost as useless to its members as the situation of ten men on the ice floe sharing substarvation rations." John Hospers, *Human Conduct* (New York: Harcourt, Brace & World, 1961), p. 428. (This and the following excerpts from John Hospers, *Human Conduct*, are reprinted with the permission of the publisher.) On the conception of a utility floor, see also B. de Jouvenel, *The Ethics of Redistribution*, pp. 23–24 and 85–88.

9 E. Halévy, *The Growth of Philosophic Radicalism*, tr. Mary Morris, p. 502.

10 For a detailed historical and ethical treatment of the living-wage concept, see John A. Ryan, *A Living Wage* (New York: Macmillan, 1906; 2nd edn., 1920).

3. *An Equity Principle Is Needed*

But the amendment proposed in the preceding section will not of itself suffice. For even when one inserts such a "utility floor" for the purpose of catastrophe-prevention, one does not provide for cases of the following sort. We have now to do with five people, Messrs *A, B, C, D,* and *E,* whose respective utility shares for two schemes of distribution are represented by (a), (b), (c), (d), and (e).

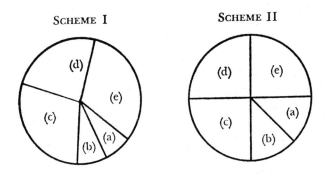

Let it be supposed that the acceptable minimal level is just exactly represented by the shares (a) and (b) on Scheme I, so that there is no question of anyone's being pressed "beneath the floor." Also the *total amounts* of utility (represented by the sizes of the two circles) may be supposed to be the same. Now the principle of utility dictates the preferability of Scheme I, since it assumes "the greater good of the greater number" of persons involved, viz., the recipients of shares (c)–(e). But even a rudimentary sensitivity to equity and justice revolts against this conclusion. For why should the hapless recipients of shares (a)–(b) be pressed to the floor in order to make the "rich" who receive (c)–(e) yet richer?

What is clearly needed, over and above the aforementioned

utility floor, is some added principle of equity in the distribution of utility shares, some reference to the central tendency of
utility allocations that will take equitableness into account. A
reasonable (and in other contexts familiar) procedure might
be *a rule of least square deviation from the average.* The
adoption of such an equity principle would iron out difficulties of the type illustrated by the previous example.

Consider such a case as that of choosing between giving
Messrs *A, B, C, D,* and *E* one of the following utility
distributions:

Share	SCHEME I	SCHEME II
(a)	7 units	6 units
(b)	7	6
(c)	7	6
(d)	2	10
(e)	2	12

From the angle of *total* utility, Scheme II is superior. But
Scheme I gives "the greater number" of persons (viz., 3 of
them) a greater utility share than they would have in Scheme
II. Also, from the standpoint of central tendency, Scheme I is
superior (the sum of the squares of deviations from the average is 30 for Scheme I but 32 for Scheme II). But, on the other
hand, in adopting Scheme II in place of Scheme I, Messrs *A,
B,* and *C* are each made to undergo *a trivially small sacrifice
in utility in order that a substantial benefit can accrue to* D
and E. It is clear that *if the claims of the individuals concerned are equal,* Scheme II is definitely to be preferred.[11]

Consider the alternative schemes of utility allocation in

[11] The point that we may prefer the distribution of a lesser total with
greater equality is developed with force and clarity in John Hospers,
Human Conduct, pp. 428–429. It is, of course, based on a fundamental
commitment diametrically opposed to the hard-nosed maximize-the-
total-and-distribution-be-damned line of utilitarianism espoused by
F. Y. Edgeworth, who held that J. S. Mill "darkens the subject (as many
critics seem to have felt), by imposing a condition of equality of distribution" (*Mathematical Psychics,* p. 118.)

which Messrs $X, Y,$ and Z get shares (a), (b), and (c), respectively:

Share	SCHEME I	SCHEME II
(a)	5 units	9 units
(b)	6	1 (= the "floor")
(c)	10	12

Note that Scheme II represents the greater good (22 units as compared with 21), and represents a greater good for a greater number (viz., Messrs X and Z are comparative beneficiaries in its adoption). But is Scheme II unqualifiedly preferable and its selection morally mandatory—regardless of who it is that is doing the selecting? (We tend to react differently if the choice of the second scheme is made by Y rather than by X.[12] The doctrinaire utilitarian has to write this difference in reaction off to foolish sentimentality.) Actually, the adoption of an equity principle of the sort under discussion would rationalize the selection of the first—patently fairer—allocation scheme. One could implement the principle by introducing the idea of an "effective average" which would discount the actual average by some function of the deviations from it (say by half of the standard deviation[13]). The concept of an effective average will be treated in greater detail in the next section.

It deserves to be stressed again at this point that we are dealing with distributions of "utility" viewed retrospectively, and not with distributions of some storable good viewed prospectively. In the distributions we are concerned with there is (by hypothesis) no question of redistribution (utility cannot be alienated or transferred, and even if it could, this would be precluded by our retroactive approach). This is important, because in ruling out redistributions we also rule out mutual agreements to reallocate in the common interest. If we

12 Compare W. D. Ross, *Foundations of Ethics*, pp. 72, 75.
13 This formula would yield an effective average of 5.9 for Scheme I and of 5.8 for Scheme II.

were dealing with, say, money rather than utility, then consider, in this changed light, the case of a choice between giving Messrs *A, B,* and *C* shares (a), (b), and (c), respectively:

Share	SCHEME I	SCHEME II
(a)	3 units	10 units
(b)	3	1
(c)	3	1

Our own preference on the basis of the preceding discussion is for Scheme I (where the "effective average" is 3) over Scheme II ("effective average" is 1.9). But, of course, if redistribution were possible, *A* would work out a "mutual assistance pact" with *B* and *C* to make a payoff of 3 units to each of them for going along with the adoption of Scheme II, thereby in effect bringing into the picture

Share	SCHEME III
(a)	4 units
(b)	4
(c)	4

which is clearly preferable to either of the preceding schemes by *any* reasonable standard (ours not excluded). The distributor who would adopt Scheme II over against I with a view to laying the basis for a shift to III could plausibly be said to serve the interests of distributive justice. The considerations upon which our preference for I over II is based must be understood to include the ruling out of such a shift to (the nonenvisaged) alternative III.

In this way, it may be seen that the considerations of our discussion—while not in principle restricted to "utility," but applicable more generally—rest essentially on the stipulation that the set of alternative distributions under comparative evaluation be postulated as complete, without any widening of the range of alternatives by the possibility of redistribution.

4. The Concept of an Effective Average

In the preceding section we introduced the concept of an effective average (EA):

EA = average − $\frac{1}{2}$ σ (standard deviation from the average)

The role of this concept is simple: paradigmatically, it is to systematize the intuitive feeling that of the two distributions

Share	SCHEME I	SCHEME II
(a)	2 units	1 unit
(b)	2	1
(c)	2	3
(d)	2	3
(e)	2	3

Scheme I is superior from the angle of distributive justice to Scheme II, this being so despite the facts (1) that Scheme I yields a lesser average share (2 as contrasted with 2.2 units) and (2) that in contrasting Scheme I with Scheme II, there are two 1-unit losers as compared with three 1-unit gainers, so that Scheme II yields the greater good of a greater number. From the standpoint of our "effective average," however, the advantage lies with Scheme I (2.00 as contrasted with 1.71). The purpose of this section is to exhibit some significant features of this concept of an effective average.

The key feature of the effective average as a criterion for comparison is that it can underwrite the preferability of one distribution to another without requiring that the preferred distribution be a Pareto improvement upon its competitor. Moreover, it provides a systematic grounding for two seemingly competing intuitions as to the nature of distributive justice, viz., that in certain cases inequalities can "pay for themselves" by resulting in a situation that conduces to the general good, and, moreover, that "a lower average income, with greater equality, may make a happier society than a higher average income with less." [14] An example of the second sort of situation has just been provided. An illustration of the first sort of situation is:

Share	SCHEME I	SCHEME II
(a)	3 units	2.9 units
(b)	3	4
(c)	3	4
(d)	3	4
(e)	3	4

One qualification must immediately be made. The EA is a meaningful basis of comparison, and should in fact be regarded as being defined, only when it is not too far removed from the average—say, when EA lies within 50 per cent of the actual average A. This means that we must have

$$EA \geq \tfrac{1}{2} A$$

or equivalently, since $EA = A - \tfrac{1}{2} \sigma$ (where σ = the standard deviation from the average), we must have

$$\sigma \leq A$$

that is, the standard deviation from the average is no larger than the average itself. Only under this condition should the conception of an "effective average" be applied. Thus such distributions as

Share	SCHEME I	SCHEME II
(a)	0 units	0 units
(b)	0	1
(c)	3	8

would have no EA on this basis. In the case of very uneven distributions, when an EA is not defined, other tools must be employed. We shall not pursue the matter further here.

[14] R. H. Tawney, *Equality* (4th edn., London: Allen & Unwin, 1952), p. 129. The concept of an effective average thus serves (but more effectively) the same equalizing purpose that is served by the idea of a (utility) *ceiling*, in analogy with that of a *floor*, introduced by B. de Jouvenel. See his *The Ethics of Redistribution*, pp. 23–28, 86–87.

Compare the distributions:

Share	SCHEME I	SCHEME II	SCHEME III	SCHEME IV
(a)	2 units	0 units	x units	3 units
(b)	2	3	3	3
(c)	2	3	3	3

It is reasonably plain on the basis of intuitive considerations that Scheme I is preferable to Scheme II (since it divides the same total more equitably) and that Scheme IV is preferable to Scheme I (since everyone fares uniformly better by it). Now when $x = 0$, then III = II; and when $x = 3$, then III = IV. The question thus arises: As x is increased from 0 to 3, at what value of x does III become preferable to I? Our EA calculation yields this value as $x = 1.24$. The reader is invited to measure this result against his own intuitions, realizing that in such a matter, as elsewhere, intuition is not a precision instrument yielding exact results.

An interesting use of the concept of an effective average is its application to the analysis of income distribution data. Consider the tabulation given below, derived from two sources: (1) U. S. Bureau of the Census, *Historical Statistics of the United States* (Washington, D.C., 1960), and (2) *idem., Statistical Abstract of the United States*, 86th edn. (Washington, D.C., 1965):

Average income for families and
unattached individuals in the USA
(In 1,000's of 1950 dollars)

	ACTUAL AVERAGE		EFFECTIVE AVERAGE	
YEAR	*Amount*	*% increase over 1929*	*Amount*	*% increase over 1929*
1929	3.36	0	1.61	0
1941	3.66	9%	1.81	12%
1950	4.44	32%	2.33	45%
1962	5.78	72%	3.10	93%

The fact of a significant disparity in the distribution of income is revealed by the discrepancy between the actual and the effective average. On the other hand, the comparative lessening of this disparity is indicated by the significantly more rapid increase of the effective average as compared with the actual average.

Our contention is that an EA measure of this sort, when defined, appears to provide a good basis of comparison, and thus an acceptable solution of the "meshing problem" in the relative assessment of the merit of greater or lesser *amounts* versus greater or lesser *equity* in alternative distributions.

5. The Need for a Solution to the "Meshing Problem"

In the face of the considerations adduced so far, it might seem plausible to adopt the *maximin criterion* of choice, giving preference to that alternative distribution which has the largest minimum share.[15] But consider the following two distribution schemes (with, say, 1 unit as the utility "floor"):

Share	SCHEME I	SCHEME II
(a)	1.9 units	7 units
(b)	3.1	3
(c)	3	2
(d)	3	2
(e)	3	2
(f)	3	2
(g)	3	2

Scheme II has the greater minimum, but is, pretty obviously, not to be preferred to Scheme I.[16]

[15] This is not a version but a revision of utilitarianism. Its sole advocate known to me is (apparently) Marcus G. Singer. See pp. 202–203 of his *Generalization in Ethics* (New York: Alfred A. Knopf, 1961).

[16] An analogous counterexample will serve against the *minimax criterion* that minimizes the maximum. A somewhat greater (but still finite)

Suppose we are confronted with the choice between two alternative schemes of utility allocation, as follows: [17]

Share	SCHEME I	SCHEME II
Made very happy	30 people	20 people
Made fairly happy	20	40
Made rather unhappy	45	35
Made very unhappy (i.e., pushed "below the floor")	5	5

Here, if Scheme I is adopted, the total number of happy people is decreased by 10, as compared with Scheme II, but the number of people made very happy is increased comparably. It is clear that *if the claims of the individuals are equal* we are still confronted with a possible conflict between "greater good" on the one hand and "greater number" on the other. For the orthodox utilitarian, this gap remains to be bridged— or perhaps simply faced and accepted as irresolvable at the theoretical level.

The problem was stated with model clarity by John Hospers in his ethics textbook:

> The twentieth-century utilitarians . . . have always interpreted the classical utilitarians as meaning that one should aim at the largest total quantity of intrinsic good, with no qualifications or additions saying that quantity of good is to be sacrificed when a more nearly equal distribution can thereby be achieved. (Why then did Bentham and Mill include the phrase "for the greatest number"? Probably to insure that every person was included in the calculations of the greatest total quantity.) Our problem, then, is this: does this classical utilitarian account of the matter (largest total quantity of good, with everybody

---

amount of ingenuity is needed to provide a counterexample to the maximin-cum-minimax combination of these two principles.

[17] I adapt this example from A. C. Ewing, "Political Differences," *The Philosophical Quarterly*, XIII (1963), 333–343 (see p. 338). Note that the numbers here represent numbers of people, and not utility units as in preceding charts.

being figured into the total) need revision in the light of the principle of equal distribution which we have said is included in our idea of justice?

Most thoughtful people, it seems, desire both ideals to be achieved: they would like to have a society in which the largest total *amount* of good is present, and if they had to choose between a society containing more good and a society containing less, they would unhesitatingly choose the first. Similarly, however, they would like to have a society in which good is, as nearly as possible, *equally distributed* (with exceptions we shall take up in the next section) ; and if they had to choose between a society in which good was equally distributed and one in which there were glaring inequalities, they would choose the first. The question is, what is to be done when the two ideals conflict? Are we—as the classical utilitarians would say. or at any rate as we are taking them to mean—always to select the alternative that contains the maximum total quantity of good, irrespective of its distribution? Or are we, as the supporters of justice would say, to select the alternative that contains the most nearly equal distribution of good, regardless of the amount? Or are we somehow to mediate between the two views by considering *both* principles and by believing that the right act should embody them both—the greatest total possible good that is compatible with the most nearly equal distribution thereof? It is probably fair to say that most people, once they have thought of it, would consider the third alternative—the one bringing in both principles—to be the best.[18]

This "meshing problem" of balancing the total amount of good at issue in a given putative distribution against the fairness of the distribution in cases where these two desiderata cut against one another is one which utilitarians (and nonutilitarians, for that matter) have never resolved satisfactorily. However, its analysis seems to be a pressing task for an adequate substantive theory of distributive justice. Our proposed concept of an *effective average* is offered as a tentative step toward its solution. Be this as it may, the analysis has, I believe, established one important and essentially negative re-

[18] John Hospers, *Human Conduct*, p. 426. Note that any such defect in the utilitarian principle of distribution affects the rule-version just as much as the act-version of the theory.

sult. The principle of utility cannot of itself play the part of a
final arbiter in a selection among alternative distributions.
The application of the principle involves choices among alternatives whose resolution requires recourse to a further and at
least equally fundamental principle. As Sidgwick already
clearly saw (see pp. 51–52, below), the principle of utility fails
us in its purported role as an ultimate recourse because we
cannot avoid choices among alternative modes of implement-
ing the utilitarian principle itself, choices, therefore, of such
a character that they cannot in the nature of things be settled
by the principle itself.

6. The Question of Claims

Thus far we have emphasized what might be called the domes-
tic difficulties of the principle of utility (greater good *versus*
greater number). But there are also its foreign difficulties vis-à-
vis the concepts of fairness and equity. These may be illustrated by contrasting the following two utility allocations:

Share	SCHEME I	SCHEME II
(a)	4 units	4 units
(b)	4	3
(c)	4	3
(d)	1	2

From the orthodox utilitarian standpoint, all the advantages
lie with Scheme I: (i) It represents the greater *total* good (13
contrasted with 12 units) and the greater *average* good (3.25
as contrasted with 3.00 units). (ii) It represents a "greater
good for a greater number" since two individuals are beneficiaries (1-unit beneficiaries) of its adoption and only one
individual is the loser (1-unit loser) thereby. But on the other
hand, *supposing that the individuals who are to be recipients*

of these four shares all have equal claims, a very positive point of merit on the part of Scheme II must be recognized: it is significantly more equitable.[19] If one is prepared, in cases such as this, to give weight to the fairness of distributions, even when this goes against the factors operative in the principle of utility ("greater good," "greater number"), one is, in effect, abandoning this principle as the ultimate arbiter in matters of distributive justice by introducing a wholly new consideration of which the principle takes no account.

The point we are making here is certainly not new, being one of the standard objections to utilitarianism on the part of nineteenth-century critics. Herbert Spencer put the matter as follows:

"Everybody to count for one, nobody for more than one." Does this mean that, in respect of whatever is proportioned out, each is to have the same share whatever his character, whatever his conduct? Shall he if passive have as much as if active? Shall he if useless have as much as if useful? Shall he if criminal have as much as if virtuous? If the distribution is to be made without reference to the natures and deeds of the recipients, then it must be shown that a system which equalizes, as far as it can, the treatment of good and bad, will be beneficial. If the distribution is not to be indiscriminate, then the

[19] For Scheme I, the sum of the squares of the deviations from the average is 6.75. For Scheme II this factor only amounts to 2. The "effective average" for Scheme I is 2.60 contrasted with 2.65 for Scheme II. As a matter of incidental interest, it is worth noting that if this same general pattern of the distribution at issue is extended to involve a greater number of other people, the type-I distribution becomes preferable. For example, contrast:

Share	SCHEME I	SCHEME II
(a)	4 units	4 units
(b)	4	3
(c)	4	3
(d)	4	3
(e)	4	3
(f)	1	2

Now Scheme I is preferable to II since its *effective average* is the larger (2.9 as against 2.7).

formula disappears. The something distributed must be apportioned otherwise than by equal division. There must be adjustment of amounts to deserts; and we are left in the dark as to the mode of adjustment—we have to find other guidance.[20]

In the case of an unequal group of claims, the difficulties grow more acute than ever. Here we would in general have to confront a given schedule of (legitimate) claims and a set of alternative distributions among which to effect a (rationally defensible) preferential selection. An example would be as follows:

Individuals involved	Schedule of claims	ALTERNATIVE DISTRIBUTIONS		
		SCHEME I	SCHEME II	SCHEME III
A	4	5 units	8 units	1 unit
B	4	5	4	5
C	8	6	4	10

In such a case we would (at any rate as long as the total amounts being distributed are the same [21]) clearly prefer that distribution which has the least sum of squares-of-differences-from-the-schedule, that is, Scheme I in the example. But what in the case of a tie by this criterion, as in the example:

Individuals	Claims	DISTRIBUTIONS	
		SCHEME I	SCHEME II
A	2	3 units	0 units
B	3	1	4
C	4	2	2

Here we would surely prefer the intrinsically more equitable distribution, that is, the one with the larger effective average—i.e., Scheme I.

The standpoint at which we have thus arrived supports the

20 Herbert Spencer, *The Data of Ethics* (New York: D. Appleton & Co., 1879), sec. 84.
21 Cases in which this condition is not satisfied are treated in ch. 5.

charge of shortcomings that we had earlier found it necessary to make against the utilitarian standard for assessing distributions. The principle is involved in an internal fission which leads to the need for further choices in its application in certain cases. These choices, being choices that arise in the *application of* the utilitarian principle, cannot be settled by the principle itself. They require an outside appeal—to such concepts as equity or fairness in accommodating claims—and in this way point to the fact that the utilitarian standard must be viewed as representing one factor among others. It simply will not do to regard the principle of utility as an ultimate and complete basis for a theory of distributive justice. Furthermore, we have found the direction in which one must look to find those necessary further factors of distributive justice, namely, considerations of equity in the accommodation of claims.[22] The focus of attention must thus shift to this matter of claims.

[22] When Saint Paul wrote "Masters, give unto your servants that which is just and equal" (Colossians 4:1), the "equal" at issue is not to be construed as "equal to what all the others get" but as "equal to his deserts."

3

Legitimate Claims

1. The Problem of Claims and Desert

If the claims of the individuals concerned are equal: an absolutely crucial, and to this point wholly ignored, cluster of considerations lurks in this clause.

Let us suppose Mr. *A* to be the very personification of virtue and Mr. *B* the embodiment of vice. And consider two schemes of utility allocation giving these two individuals the shares (a) and (b) respectively:

SCHEME I   SCHEME II

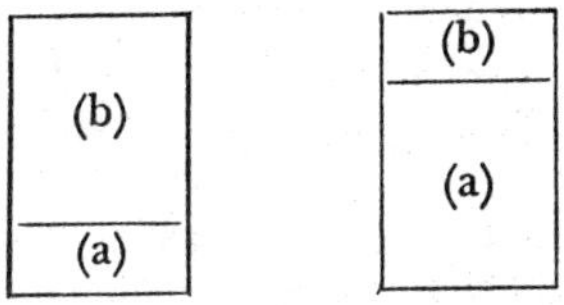

On the basis of the principle of utility above, taking account only of the total utility and the arithmetic of its distribution, there is nothing whatever to choose between these schemes. This upshot is patently unpalatable from a moral standpoint.

But worse is yet to come. Let us add to the *dramatis personae* of the preceding example also a Mr. *C*, who puts Mr. *B* quite into the shade in point of nastiness. Consider now the utility-allocation schemes:

Share	SCHEME I	SCHEME II
(a)	4 units	1 unit
(b)	2	2
(c)	1	5

If the principle of utility is our sole guide, there is patently nothing to do but adopt Scheme II in preference to its alternative. Crude and unreconstructed utilitarianism thus seems prepared to do substantial violence to elemental considerations of justice and common-sense morality.

From this standpoint it becomes clear that the *decisive and fatal* objection to any straightforward adoption of the classical principle of utility as a rule of distribution is this: it leaves wholly out of account that essential reference to claims, merit, and desert without which no theory of distributive justice fulfills the requisite for serious consideration.[1] In taking into account only the characteristics of the distribution of goods—"greatest good," "greatest number"—naive utilitarianism (and unsophisticated welfare economics) decisively to its detriment rides roughshod over the distinguishing claims of individuals. The emphasis of the "intuitionist" and "deontologist" opponents of classical utilitarianism upon the moral sense of justice was (as we see it) thoroughly well placed.[2]

2. *The Classical Utilitarians on Claims*

Utilitarians have realized from the beginning that justice could prove a stumbling block in the path of their theory. Bentham himself wrote:

> But justice, what is it that we are to understand by justice: and why not happiness but justice? What happiness is, every man

[1] The point is cogently urged by W. D. Ross in *Foundations of Ethics*, pp. 76–77. No one, of course, denies that the classical utilitarians made—from the very start—certain rudimentary allowances for the principle of justice; as in Bentham's formula, "everybody to count for one, and nobody for more than one."

[2] A thoroughgoing dyed-in-the-wool utilitarian (such as J. J. C. Smart?) would of course not look at the matter in this light. For him what we regard as the deliverances of "the moral sense of justice" are but the misguided intimations of outmoded sentimentality. As Smart put the matter in correspondence: "Someone who feels strongly that the utilitarian principle is correct will of course judge our commonsense moral feelings by the principle, not vice-versa."

knows, because, what pleasure is, every man knows, and what pain is, every man knows. But what justice is—this is what on every occasion is the subject-matter of dispute. Be the meaning of the word *justice* what it will, what regard is it entitled to otherwise than as a means to happiness.[3]

Justice, according to Bentham, is an inherently obscure notion that must not be permitted to retard the pursuit of happiness.[4]

Classical utilitarians (in particular, Mill), ever fully alive to difficulties of this sort, struggled manfully with their resolution. Their argument, in brief, was as follows: "If goods are distributed unjustly, the 'normal expectations' of men are frustrated and the natural order of society undermined, with a resulting detriment to the general good." An unjust distribution, it is argued, is one that may in some cases seem to serve utilitarian purposes but cannot in the nature of things actually do so: the unjust can never be truly utile. We may therefore regard justice as naturally derivative from utility and subordinate to it.

It is interesting to observe that this line of argument is an exact counterpart to Cicero's attempt (in our motto from *De officiis*) to subordinate utility (expediency) to justice. An unjust act, he argues, can merely *seem* expedient, but cannot in the nature of things actually be so: the truly utile can never be unjust. We may therefore regard utility as naturally derivative from justice and subordinate to it.

Both lines of argumentation fall back upon essentially the same specious distinction between a *true* utility that must square with justice and a merely *seeming* utility that may be in conflict with it. Both positions take comfort in the same comforting illusion that "in the final analysis," utility and justice must—somehow—come to terms of agreement.

3 Bentham, *Constitutional Code*, ch. 16, sec. 6.
4 But compare Herbert Spencer's cogent objection that the history of this subject indicates no greater (and possibly less) consensus regarding the meaning of *happiness* than of *justice* (*The Data of Ethics*, sec. 60).

Suppose we look at a distribution from the retrospective angle—with the supposition that "all returns are in," and that *all the correct allowances have been made* for frustrations, disappointments, etc.—and that *then* we are to choose between the two alternative schemes for a utility allocation among 100 persons:

	SCHEME I			SCHEME II	
	Persons made happy	Persons made unhappy		Persons made happy	Persons made unhappy
"Deserving"	0	10	"Deserving"	70	5
"Undeserving"	90	0	"Undeserving"	5	20

Surely the naively utilitarian espousal of Scheme I violates our natural sense of justice.

The classical utilitarians are on the side of the angels on this issue: they yield to no one in their eagerness to give considerations of justice and desert their appropriate weight. Their error, I believe, is not one of wrongheadedness, but— prior to Sidgwick—of self-delusion in convincing themselves that this desideratum can somehow be derived as a *strict consequence* of the principle of utility. The position of orthodox utilitarianism on this point was already taken up by that proto-utilitarian (indeed rule-utilitarian) David Hume, who argued at great length and with great fervor that "the rules of equity or justice depend entirely on the particular state and condition, in which men are placed, and owe their origin and existence to that UTILITY, which results to the public from their strict and regular observance" so that "the necessity of justice to the support of society is the SOLE foundation of that virtue." [5]

Sidgwick faced the problem squarely:

[5] In Section III, "Of Justice," and Appendix II of *An Enquiry Concerning the Principles of Morals;* compare also Part II of Book III, "Of Justice and Injustice," of the *Treatise of Human Nature.*

> It is evident that there are many different ways of distributing the same quantum of happiness among the same number of persons; in order, therefore, that the utilitarian criterion of right conduct may be as complete as possible, we ought to know which of these ways is to be preferred. . . . Now the Utilitarian formula seems to supply no answer to this question: at least we have to supplement the principle of seeking the greatest happiness on the whole by some principle of Just or Right distribution of this happiness. The principle which most Utilitarians have either tacitly or expressly adopted is that of pure equality. . . . [6]

What Sidgwick fails to stress with the emphasis it demands is that such a recourse to a principle of justice is not a matter of removing a minor incompleteness in the principle of utility, but the introduction of another, importantly new type of consideration that can even cut against considerations of utility and that requires systematic coordination with the principle of utility. To hold Sidgwick's position consistently requires not a supplementation, but an *abandonment* of the classical, one-track utilitarianism.[7]

One must distinguish between the immanent and the transeunt goodness of alternative distributions of any type of good. Its *immanent* (or internal) goodness is determined by the goodness or merit of the entire distribution itself (i.e., the goodness of the pattern of distribution). Analogously, the *immanent* goodness of a hypothetical universe is fixed by the amount of the goodness *in* it, and its *transeunt* goodness is fixed by the amount of the goodness *of* it. And, as our examples have shown, these two things are not to be identified.[8] Indeed, it is crucial for the theory of distributive justice that

---

[6] *The Methods of Ethics,* Book IV, ch. 1, sec. 2.

[7] Actually, Sidgwick's principal departure from the utilitarian position is in the direction of egoism, in adding a principle of self-interest to the utilitarian principle of public interest.

[8] The distinction was clearly drawn by C. D. Broad, *Five Types of Ethical Theory,* p. 252.

they be kept carefully distinct. Yet defenses of the utilitarian theory sometimes slip over from one kind of goodness to the other. Even G. E. Moore (in Section Seventeen of *Principia Ethica*) moves from "It will increase the goodness *of* the world if I do X rather than not" to "It will increase the goodness *in* the world if I do X rather than not." (Only thus does he obtain his principle [Section Eighty-nine] that "The assertion, 'I am morally bound to perform this action' is identical with the assertion, 'This action will produce the greatest possible amount of good in the universe.' ") Moore is able to lay to rest the difficulties which immediately crop up only by means of his "principle of organic unity," which justifies the claim that the goodness *in the universe as a whole* need not be correlated in any fixed way with the goodness *in the several constituent elements of the universe.* In this way he is able to salvage the needed distinction between immanent and transeunt goodness. As against this principle of Moore's, our direct emphasis on the merit of distributions avoids any (unsought for and unwarranted) inference that somehow the goodness of the present in whole may be secured at the expense of that present in the parts, and that in distinguishing between immanent and transeunt goodness we are moving in the direction of a doctrine of something akin to *raison d'état.*

3. *Claim-Equalization*

But cannot the utilitarian principle be reformulated so as to meet this line of objection? Let it be admitted that the original formulation of the principle contains a hidden assumption. It tacitly supposes that *the individuals at issue are indifferent in respect of claims*—that their merit is the same, that their desert regarding the allocation of utility is identical.

There seems to be little harm in this if viewed as a limiting restriction for the applicability of the principle. (No harm, that is, for anything other than the serviceability of the principle of utility, which now becomes even in principle confined to a very restricted group of cases.) Viewed as an assumption about "the way things are," it of course does gross violence to the facts of life.

Cannot the utilitarian principle of distribution readily be patched up to take account of the legitimate claims of the individuals concerned? Suppose that some amount of a good is to be divided among several persons: what part of it can Mr. X legitimately lay claim to as his portion? The principle of utility provides a ready answer (but only one). It is this: Consider the share that falls to X's lot in that distribution which achieves the objective of assuring "the greatest good of the greatest number," and then take as X's proper share his share in *this* distribution. (If there are several such distributions, I would suppose that X cannot on the basis of the principle of utility properly *claim* more than the minimum of his alternative shares.)

But this is paper-towel reasoning: it won't wash. For with this view of claims, it does not help the utilitarian one jot to take claims into account. It is clear that the proportioning of shares to claims leaves exactly the *status quo ante* when the claims are tailored to fit the shares. There would be a vitiating circularity in the procedure of doling out claims as determined in terms of the public interest—that is, by considerations of utility—and then going on to maintain that we utilitarians accommodate justice by satisfying claims.

4. *The Role of Deservingness*

Even with the indicated claim-equalization assumption, the principle of utilitarianism continues to be in difficulties. For consider the following alternative divisions of utility shares among three *thoroughly but equally undeserving* individuals of exactly identical status with respect to claims:

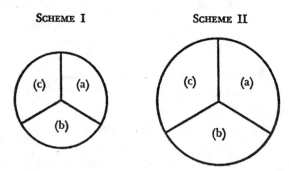

SCHEME I   SCHEME II

It seems clear to me that common sense would balk at the principle of utility's (automatic) option for Scheme II.

The doctrinaire utilitarian's insistence upon the maximization of happiness as the sole and exclusive consideration is misguided. Would many reasonable men prefer to our world another just exactly like it except in one sole respect—that Adolf Hitler's share of happiness is larger (at no one's expense)? [9] And yet this hypothetical world answers precisely to the utilitarian's prescript of a "greater happiness of a greater number." Unreconstructed utilitarianism is surely wrong at this point: happiness maximization (or utility maximization) is not a good in itself—and certainly does not serve the interests of justice—regardless of *how* it is maximized. One has to build into the principle of utility not only an equal claims qualification, but also the qualification that the individuals involved are all "deserving."

I have heard the following objection: "But the example is one in which the deprivation of happiness *ex hypothesi* serves

[9] Note that *punishment* is not at issue here, for it is the specific infliction of unpleasantness in response to an act of wrongdoing that the subject has committed, and must therefore be part of the causal sequence of developments.

no purpose, such as making others happier from *Schaden-freude,* or leading an evildoer to 'mend his ways,' or 'serving as a lesson' *pour encourager les autres.* Surely, however, one must endorse the principle that there should be as much happiness as possible in the world, unless some definite constructive purpose is served by its diminution." The principle is plausible but does not cut against the case in hand, for a constructive purpose *is* present here, viz., "to make the world a juster one." [10] Happiness in our view is not an unconditional good, regardless of how arrived at. Suppose *A* inflicts an injury upon *B.* There is an act *X* which prevents the (otherwise automatic) penalty upon *A*—thus increasing the total happiness in the world—but (be it supposed) has no other causal effects upon the welfare of men. The performance of the act *X* would then, in our view, be a deed of saintly merit *if done by B,* but one of near-demonic demerit if done by some "outsider" *C.*[11]

5. *Shares Must Be Based upon Claims*

However ardently one may espouse the dictum that "all men are created equal," i.e., come into the world with exactly the

---

[10] J. S. Mill was (I think) prepared to concede this point: " . . . it is universally considered just that each person should obtain that (whether good or evil) which he *deserves;* and unjust that he should obtain a good, or be made to undergo an evil, which he does not deserve. This is, perhaps, the clearest and most emphatic form in which the idea of justice is conceived by the general mind. As it involves the notion of desert, the question arises, what constitutes desert? Speaking in a general way, a person is understood to deserve good if he does right, evil if he does wrong; and in a more particular sense, to deserve good from those to whom he does or has done good, and evil from those to whom he does or has done evil. The precept of returning good for evil has never been regarded as a case of the fulfillment of justice, but as one in which the claims of justice are waived, in obedience to other considerations." *Utilitarianism,* ch. 5.

[11] On this point, compare W. D. Ross, *The Right and the Good,* p. 22.

same status regarding claims, merit, and desert, there is no
gainsaying that this situation is radically altered once men
begin to act. Human actions—or at any rate, the great bulk of
them—are inherently claim-modifying: they bring into being
assets and liabilities, and engender merit and demerit. Surely
nobody would want to hold that when the prize is to be
awarded, there is no difference in the claims of the winner and
the losers. Surely nobody would want to say that when the
payroll is disbursed, the employer should be governed by the
rule of "the greatest happiness of the greatest number," indifferent to the question of who are his workmen and who are
not. Life is replete with "claim-creating circumstances" typified by the making (and breaking) of promises and contracts;
in the nature of things, most distributions are of the functional sort that is unavoidably claim-responsive. "The greatest
good of the greatest number, *always recognizing that the resulting distribution of goods and evils should be commen-
surate with the legitimate claims of the individuals at issue*"
—surely some such "proportionality qualification" is crucial
and cannot be dispensed with. The "principle of utility" cannot be a serious candidate for a principle of distribution when
its formulation does not take account of the desert (merit,
legitimate claims) of the individuals involved.

In a fundamental sense the concept of justice involves that
of proportion: *congruitas ac proportionalitas quaedam*.[12] Discussions of distributive justice cannot ignore Aristotle's emphasis[13] that in a just distribution, shares must be proportioned to desert or merit (*kata axian*) in terms of the relevant
claims of the respective recipients.[14]

---

[12] *Leibniz: Juris ac aequi elementa*, in *Mitteilungen aus Leibnizens unge-
druckten Schriften*, ed. G. Mollat (Leipzig, 1893), pp. 22 ff.
[13] *Nicomachean Ethics* V. 5, 1130b31–33, and V. 6, 1131a20–27. Cf. W. D.
Ross, *Aristotle* (5th edn.), pp. 210–211.
[14] "It is often held by theologians that in the next world all the accounts
will be set straight, that everyone will receive just what he deserves,
and that therefore there will be 'perfect justice.' Kant, in fact, used

In taking this position, we must avoid tempting misunderstandings. It is *not* being said that it is not just to pay a debt to a morally wicked person. (The indebtedness is wholly definitive of the claims at issue, and the moral character of the creditor is entirely irrelevant to these claims.) Nor is it being said that the state is not to treat all as "equal before the law," but should accord preferential treatment to morally superior individuals. (As long as its subjects comport themselves within "the limits of the law," it is perfectly appropriate for the state to regard their moral character as irrelevant in point of claim-establishment as regards the sorts of distributions at issue.) In short, it is to be stressed that our thesis that *a just distribution must be based upon claims* is to be construed in such a way that the *legitimate claims* in question are relevant and appropriate with respect to the distribution at issue.

What is the "Pure Principle of Distributive Justice?" According to a formula once proposed by Sidgwick, justice is the similar and injustice the dissimilar treatment of similars. But *this* formulation of an "equity principle" as being merely a matter of adherence to the rule *Treat likes alike!* is clearly inadequate, because it encompasses only a part of the story. Let us consider six persons: A_1 and A_2 both very (but equally) undeserving, B_1 and B_2 both highly (but equally) deserving, and C_1 and C_2 both moderately deserving. And let us consider a distribution that allocates to A_1 and A_2 large (but equal) shares of utility, to C_1 and C_2 modest (equal) shares, and to B_1 and B_2 both minute (and equal) shares. Obviously this distribution satisfies the injunction of a similar treatment of similars, but it is, just as obviously, grossly unjust. The "equity principle" under consideration must be

---

this position as an argument for immortality: the moral law requires justice (apportionment of reward to desert), and in this world justice often does not triumph; therefore there must be a life after this one in which it does. As an argument, most philosophers agree that this one is not successful. But at least it is a testimonial to the widespread and deep-seated desire for justice." John Hospers, *Human Conduct*, pp. 433–434.

supplemented by a "proportionality principle" that the shares of the distribution be proportionate to claims.[15]

The search for a principle of justice is thus brought back to the Roman jurists' dictum that the definitive principle of justice is inherent in the dictum *suum cuique tribuere*, "to give each his own," or to Simonides' dictum *to ta opheilomena hekastōi apodidonai dikaion esti*, "to give what is owed to each is just" (see Plato, *Republic* 331d ff.). But what, from the standpoint of distributive justice, can be said to be "his own"? Plainly the answer is "what he deserves," i.e., a share ideally equal—and in any event, in general proportional—to his legitimate claims. (Even this must be adapted to the case of indivisible goods.) And of course it is not just moral deservingness in general that is at issue here, but functional deservingness determined with respect to the defining conditions of the distribution at issue.

In saying that the issue of distributive justice cannot be properly broached, let alone resolved, without taking *claims* into account, we must not be interpreted as holding that the claims at issue are merely the purely legal claims and "rights" enshrined in positive law. Here, as elsewhere, the distinction between the merely legal and the genuinely just is operative, and the claims and rights at issue are certainly meant to include those whose foundation is of a moral rather than exclusively legal nature.

A fatal defect of naive utilitarianism is its incapacity to provide adequate accommodation for the pivotal facet of *justice*. No acceptable ethical theory can articulate its principle of choice among alternative distributions of goods and evils in abstraction from a consideration of the legitimate claims of

[15] I do not mean to suggest that Sidgwick did not recognize this fact; he certainly was well aware of it: "the proposition 'that men ought to be rewarded in proportion to their deserts' . . . would be commonly held to be the true and simple principle of distribution in any case where there are no claims arising from Contract or Custom to modify its operation" (*The Methods of Ethics*, 7th edn., p. 279).

the individuals at issue. But on utilitarian grounds, rights and duties, claims and obligations are always *sub judice* and always vulnerable. They are always insecure precisely because they are always at the mercy of utilitarian considerations. For the naive utilitarian, justice and obligation are always provisional matters, subject to possible subordination to considerations of utility.

To say this is not to deny that in many or most cases what sorts of things are to count as legitimate claims may be established by a utilitarian (i.e., rule-utilitarian) approach. What is denied is that claim-establishing considerations must inevitably pass such a utilitarian test under pain of being counted as illegitimate. Obligations are obligations, and claims, claims, in a basic and primary way, irrespective of the utilitarian expediency of honoring them as such. To use an analogy: Exactly as the utilitarian question of whether or not "honesty is the best policy" is simply irrelevant to the moral status of honesty, so the utilitarian expediency of recognizing proper claims is irrelevant to their legitimacy as claims and to the injustice of action in their despite.

But notice how far we have now departed from exclusive reliance upon the principle of utility. We have simply demoted considerations of "greatest good" and "greatest number," refusing them a preeminent status as the sole and solitary factors operative in the first instance, by coordinating them with considerations of justice. We speak advisedly of a *coordination* of considerations of utility with those of distributive justice because neither is, in our judgment, the sole ultimate criterion to which the other is to be subordinated systematically.

It is not hard to see that to hold that considerations of utility and of justice must lead to the same conclusion is to think both wishfully and carelessly. That proto-utilitarian Bernard de Mandeville illustrated graphically in his *Fable of the*

Bees that considerations of utility (general welfare) and of justice can come into head-on conflict. The uncompromising utilitarian should be prepared—with Mandeville (and perhaps J. J. C. Smart?)—to brush considerations of justice wholly aside whenever they conflict with the principle of utility. For him, justice counts only when it is serviceable as a means to the maximization of utility; in other cases it is an obstacle to be brushed conveniently aside. Anyone seriously and fundamentally committed to some principle of justice cannot be a doctrinaire utilitarian. To say this is not, of course, to say that considerations of justice must never be tempered by considerations of utility—it does not lead to that stern dictum *Fiat justitia ruat caelum,* taking but a small step in its direction. For it is crucial in this context to realize that justice has two importantly different contraries: injustice on the one hand, and on the other, that "more than justice" represented by mercy, compassion, generosity, and works of supererogation generally. It would only be in the latter category of deviations from justice that utilitarian considerations can properly be accorded room for play.

6. Our Strictures Applicable Not Only to "Act-Utilitarianism" but Also to "Rule-Utilitarianism"

The standard objection against "act-utilitarianism" (that the act to be preferred on grounds of the "greatest good of greatest number" principle may be patently improper by involving blatant violation of a moral rule—e.g., giving property entrusted for safekeeping to a needy indigent rather than restoring it to its rightful owner) applies also to rule-utilitarianism. For a rule or practice that (as best we can tell) may assure the greatest good to the greatest number may *also* be equally unacceptable in an analogous way; e.g., group punishment of persons whose "guilt" of an offense of a given type is based upon some form of association, or punishment based upon the application of *ex post facto* laws, could (very possibly) prove under specifiable sets of circumstances to be a policy of demonstrable social advantage. J. S. Mill writes: "The principle, therefore, of giving to each what they deserve, that is, good for good, as well as evil for evil, is not only included within the idea of Justice as we have defined it, but is a proper object of that intensity of sentiment which places the Just, in human estimation, above the simply Expedient." [16] What Mill fails to recognize is that this position is, in the final analysis, simply incompatible with utilitarianism—even the rule-utilitarianism he himself espouses.[17]

7. *The Grounds of Claims*

The question of how "claims" come about—how *merit* and *desert* spring into existence—seems to me among the most difficult and complex issues in ethical theory. What constitutes

---

[16] *Utilitarianism*, ch. 10.

[17] The classic exponent of the position is, of course, David Hume. Two very able recent statements of rule-utilitarianism are: S. E. Toulmin, *The Place of Reason in Ethics* (London: Cambridge University Press, 1950), and P. H. Nowell-Smith, *Ethics* (London: Penguin Books, 1954). Compare also John Rawls, "Two Concepts of Rules," *The Philosophical Review*, LXIV (1955), 3–32. For a critical discussion of rule-utilitarianism (or "restricted utilitarianism") see J. J. C. Smart, "Extreme and Restricted Utilitarianism," *The Philosophical Quarterly*, V (1956), 344–354, as well as this author's *An Outline of a System of Utilitarian Ethics* (Victoria: Melbourne University Press, 1961). Smart cogently marshals the arguments against restricted utilitarianism, and is aware of (but undaunted by) the fact that the "restricted" theory is vulnerable to rejections of the kind usually urged against the "extreme" view which the restrictions were designed to circumvent. However, the difficulties encountered by restricted utilitarianism are taken by Smart to drive us back to an extreme, unrestricted utilitarianism rather than as scoring against the utilitarian position *tout court*. The uncompromisingly anti-utilitarian position (in the manner of W. D. Ross) has found an able exponent in H. J. McCloskey, "An Examination of Restricted Utilitarianism," *The Philosophical Review*, LXVI (1957), 466–485, and "A Note on Utilitarian Punishment," *Mind*, LXXII (1963), 599.

the "merit" on the basis of which a lion's share of "utility" may legitimately be claimed?

Is it effort? Clearly not in general—the winner of a race may expend less effort than the second man in, but yet deservedly carries off the whole prize. *Is it need,* as in the Marxist slogan "to each according to his need"? Clearly not in general—as the race example again illustrates: surely the winner is not inevitably the neediest contestant. *Is it ability?* Clearly not in general—since ability can count for nothing when it is not applied usefully and properly put to work. (Think of the story of *The Tortoise and the Hare.*)

We shall later (in Chapter Four) return to a more systematic and extensive canvass of the possibilities, but for the present let these three alternatives suffice. Despite their patent inadequacy, these suggestions at least aim in the right direction: they indicate that claims must be taken into account in the interests of distributive justice, and they recognize that the subsistence of claims is not simply inherent in the human condition as such, but hinges on functional and role-relative considerations. In the final analysis, what constitutes the basis for merit is not any one single, monolithic factor at all (let alone any one *simple* thing).

The matter of legitimate claims is a many-faceted and multiform issue that ramifies through the whole of economic and moral life. A man does not simply "deserve *x*," he "deserves *x* of *Y* in virtue of *z*." Mr. *A* owes Mr. *B* a certain sum of service *s* because of certain contractual—or other—relationships between them, and not (necessarily) because *A*'s giving *s* to *B* makes the world a better place to live in. What a "fair" share is for a distributor to give to someone in a given distribution of goods is a function of the role of the recipient in the mutual relationship subsisting between them: it may (say) be one thing *qua* business partner and another *qua* brother-in-law.

Consider the actual discrepancy between the remuneration an institution gives to its least and lowliest and to its grandest and topmost employee—perhaps a factor of 7 in a university (instructor to president), of 20 in the Federal service (postman to President), of 50 in the Bethlehem Steel Corporation, and somewhat higher in the Red Army. It is surely because of the different *roles* played (or "services rendered") by the individuals in their relationship to the institution that such discrepancies are defensible (to whatever extent they are defensible—and there is surely *some* extent to which they are). Claims are not merely claims for something, but are by and large claims *upon* someone *in virtue of* some claim-establishing consideration (based in general upon some mutual relationship).[18] And a doctrine of distribution that is not predicated upon a judicious accommodation of claims is **not** a theory of distributive justice (whatever else it may be).

When is a distribution of goods (and evils) made fairly and when does a distribution act justly? In a subtle and interesting paper, John Rawls speaks of "the usual sense of justice in which it is essentially the elimination of arbitrary distinctions and the establishment. . . of a proper balance between competing claims," going on to specify that:

> inequalities are arbitrary unless it is reasonable to expect that they will work out for everyone's advantage and provided the positions and offices to which they attach, or from which they may be gained, are open to all.[19]

I shall not pause to dwell on the difficulties inherent in the notion of inequalities that will work for literally *everyone's* advantage, difficulties most readily brought out by contemplating the problem of just action in an "economy of scarcity" (where even the best possible arrangement can only benefit

18 That utilitarians neglect this feature and "simplify unduly our relations to our fellows" is ably brought out by W. D. Ross, *The Right and the Good*, p. 19.
19 "Justice as Fairness," *The Philosophical Review*, LXVII (1958), 164–194 (quotation from p. 165).

some but not all of the parties involved). Rather I want to dwell on the concept that an inequality is arbitrary if attached to a position that is not "open to all." Consider the Presidency of the United States. It is not "open to all" (e.g., persons under 35 years of age, foreign nationals, and naturalized citizens are excluded). Surely the existence of a *qualification of eligibility*—although it *ipso facto* renders the position not "open to all"—need not produce an arbitrary inequality and lead to injustice. What has to be said is (1) that the qualification criteria are relevant and legitimate in view of the character of the office, and (2) that the office is then "open to all *qualified* persons alike." But the legitimacy of qualification criteria is now seen to become the locus of difficulty. A qualification that is plausible in some contexts may be less plausible in others. We feel differently—no doubt on utilitarian grounds—about a hereditary keepership of the royal seals on the one hand and a hereditary prime ministership on the other.[20] In a cruder society in which military defense is a chief duty for most of the male citizenry, and in which women are exempt from military service, it makes some sense to deny women the right to "have a say" in the affairs of state by voting; but modern total warfare, in annihilating the line separating soldier from civilian also undermines liability to military service as a qualification criterion for the right to vote. When a difference ceases to make a difference, we cannot in justice invoke it as basis for a qualification hurdle that disqualifies some.

Is merit (desert) ever—sometimes, always—*deserved*? The question is seemingly absurd, for it might seem that merit = desert, and how can desert be deserved? But the matter is complicated, and the question is one that should at least be

[20] Rawls makes short shrift of qualification criteria which, like eligibility for kingship, rest on hereditary traits, with the *obiter dictum*: "But any offices having special benefits must be won in a fair competition in which the contestants are judged on their merits" (*Ibid.*, p. 169). But what does this do with (say) the native-born citizenship requirement for eligibility for the United States Presidency?

raised. Consider a lottery. Clearly the winner has a legitimate claim upon the prize. But does he have a legitimate claim upon *being the winner* any more than do the other contestants? Clearly not necessarily—or even usually. The problem lies in the direction of one of the most profound paradoxes of rationalizing theology:

> Let us imagine a child and a grown-up in Heaven who both died in the True Faith, but the grown-up has a higher place than the child. And the child will ask God, "Why did you give that man a higher place?" And God will answer, "He has done many good works." Then the child will say, "Why did you let me die so soon so that I was prevented from doing good?" God will answer, "I knew that you would grow up a sinner, therefore it was better that you should die a child." Then a cry goes up from the damned in the depths of Hell, "Why, O Lord, did you not let us die before we became sinners?" [21]

8. *Earned Versus Unearned Claims*

It is advisable—and for our purposes necessary—to distinguish between two types of claims (and correspondingly of claim-establishing considerations), viz., *earned* claims on the one hand, *unearned* claims on the other. Put somewhat crudely, the difference lies in that an individual secures an earned claim on the grounds of his actions and accomplishments, and secures an unearned claim on the grounds of some situational or contractual consideration, a distinction brought out by contrasting, say, the difference between an Englishman's claim to be poet laureate, on the one hand, or to be king, on the other. Earned claims have to be merited through actions—either by the actual expenditure of effort or by the inherent possession

[21] This passage is taken from the great Muslim scholastic theologian al-Ghazali (d. 1111), quoted from S. van den Bergh's Introduction to his edition of *Averroes: Tahafut al-Tahafut*, Vol. I (London: Luzac, 1954), p. x.

of some natural skill. Unearned claims—when legitimate—
devolve on an individual because of the inevitable social arrangements governing the relationships among men.[22] A child
has claims upon his parents that are not earned by what he
does, but because he is *their* child. (Incidentally, it might be
supposed that in an ideal social order, a person's unearned
claims should be rigidly proportionate to his earned claims,
but the parent-child example suffices to show the need for
qualifying this contention.)

The respective roles of earned and unearned claims in
Western social and economic life are readily made subject to
misleading analogies. The conditions of life as we know them
are neither those of a lottery, where all the claims a man has
are unearned, nor those of a race, where he comes to have
claims solely and exclusively when he earns them by application of his own efforts. The most realistic analogy is that of the
farmer whose good crop depends both upon the cooperation of
nature, in respect to which any talk of "earning" is out of the
question, and upon his own planning and exertions. Such are
the facts in the dispensation of things that lies before us, and
there seems little point in regretting that it is so. Moreover,
there is no good reason whatever to think that, in the circumstances in which we find ourselves, any improvements would
accrue to the general quality of men's lives and lots by the
systematic abolition of unearned claims.

By and large, unearned claims devolve upon persons
through contractual arrangements, though the contract involved may be—and in most plausible cases no doubt is—a
"social contract" rather than one arrived at through explicit
negotiation between the "interested parties." Certain unearned claims can be taken to be inherent in the human con-

[22] T. N. Carver (*Essays in Social Justice* [Cambridge, Mass.: Harvard University Press, 1915], p. 281) divides the "forms of income" into three
groups: earnings, stealings, and findings. Following this lead, we may
group unearned claims into two kinds, legitimate and illegitimate. Our
concern here is solely with the former category.

dition, being treated, like life and liberty, as "inalienable rights."

Consider the following illustration of how an unearned claim can come into being through contractual eventualities without any special merit on the part of the individual who has the claim.

> *X:* Please give this apple to one of the boys in your class.
>
> *Y:* But which boy?
>
> *X:* Oh, it doesn't matter.
>
> *Y:* You must be more definite about it than that.
>
> *X:* Oh, very well—give it to the tallest boy. Yes, that's it—the tallest boy. Will you do that?
>
> *Y:* Yes. I'll do it.

Consider now two possibilities for *Y*'s division of the apple between the three boys (*A*, *B*, and *C*) of his class, where *A* is the tallest, and *A*, *B*, and *C* get shares (a), (b), and (c), respectively.

Share	SCHEME I	SCHEME II
(a)	$\frac{1}{3}$ apple	1 apple
(b)	$\frac{1}{3}$	0
(c)	$\frac{1}{3}$	0

It seems clear that if *Y* adopts Scheme I, then not only can X reproach him for having undertaken something and then failed to do it, but *A* can reproach *Y* also, on grounds of not giving him something that was his due—i.e., something to which he, *A*, had a legitimate claim in view of the agreement made between *X* and *Y*. This admittedly artificial example is not to be regarded as representing a typical situation of some sort, but as making a point of general importance, namely, that it is possible for persons to acquire claims in virtue of agreements entered upon by others, to which they themselves are not in any way parties. The example thus illustrates the working rationale of the social-contract point of view, as it inheres in the instrumentality of trusteeship, i.e., agency undertaken on behalf of others. The legitimacy of claims against such trustees turns wholly on the issue of the claimant's *entitlement* irrespective of his earned *desert*.

Unearned claims of contractual character are in a large measure matters of positive law rather than abstract justice. Their legitimacy is to be supported by the modes of defense applicable to social institutions generally, prominently including appeals to utilitarian considerations lying in the direction of "the common good." Their status as *unearned* claims is wholly irrelevant to an assessment of their propriety. Think, for example, of the difference in the laws of inheritance of various countries (or various states of the United States, for that matter). Within limits they are all equally just, although they engender very different distributions of legitimate claims. It is, however, a matter of abstract justice that the legitimate claims of persons should be recognized.

9.   The Combination of Claims

Claim-establishing considerations cannot be ordered in a simple hierarchy with one broad category *en bloc* outweighing or overriding another. This fact imparts substantial interest to the question of the *combination* of claims, their meshing or mixing in the case of mutually congruent claims, and their refereeing or reconciliation in the case of mutually divergent claims. But the problem of weighing claims of one type against those of another can be very intricate, even in the relatively simple case of the diverse claims at work with respect to one and the same individual. Claims of family vs. claims of country, for example, cannot be adjudicated *en gros* as categorical units—all depends on the specific details of the cases, and the decision must sometimes go one way, sometimes another. The insight of philosophical utilitarianism was to get "utility" as the basis of comparability among incomparables, as money serves in the economics of ordinary life to provide a common basis for the relative evaluation of, say, automobiles and apples.[23] But this approach is of help at the theoretical level alone, not in actual cases; we must admit that, on the level of abstraction on which our discussion has been moving, the problem of claim adjudication and the reconciliation of conflicts of claims is one that can only be glossed over, and not dealt with properly.

[23] Here the approach of the philosophical utilitarians was no doubt different from that of their more empirically minded economist successors. From the standpoint of the economists, who sought to derive intersubjective utilities from personal choices, the philosophers' approach is to put the cart before the horse—there being no utility analogue to "the market" as an underwriter of interpersonally comparable monetary value.

4

---

*The Canons
of
Distributive
Justice
and the
Foundations
of Claims*

---

1. *The Canons of Distributive Justice*

In the course of the long history of discussions on the subject, distributive justice has been held to consist, wholly or primarily, in the treatment of all people:

1) as equals (except possibly in the case of certain "negative" distributions such as punishments).
2) according to their needs.
3) according to their ability or merit or achievements.
4) according to their efforts and sacrifices.
5) according to their actual productive contribution.
6) according to the requirements of the common good, or the public interest, or the welfare of mankind, or the greater good of a greater number.
7) according to a valuation of their socially useful services in terms of their scarcity in the essentially economic terms of supply and demand.

Correspondingly, seven "canons" of distributive justice result, depending upon which of these factors is taken as the ultimate or primary determinant of individual claims, namely, the canons of equality, need, ability, effort, productivity, public utility, and supply and demand. Brief consideration must be given to each of these proposed conceptions of justice.[1]

1 All of these canons except number 3 (the Canon of Ability) are competently and instructively discussed from an essentially economic point of view—from the special angle of the idea of a just wage or income—in ch. 14 of John A. Ryan, *Distributive Justice* (3rd edn., New York: Macmillan, 1942).

2. The Canon of Equality

This canon holds that justice consists in the treatment of people as equals. Here we have the *egalitarian* criterion of (idealistic) democratic theorists. The shortcomings of this canon have already been canvassed in considerable detail in the last chapter, to the effect that the principle is oblivious to the reality of differential claims and desert. It is vulnerable to all the same lines of objection which hold against the type of just-wage principle advocated by G. B. Shaw—to let all who contribute to the production of the social-economic product share in it equally.[2] Moreover, the specification of the exact way in which equality is to be understood is by no means so simple and straightforward as it seems on first view. Is one, for example, to think of the type of fixed constant equality that is at issue in a sales tax, or the "equal burden" type of differential equality at issue in a graduated income tax; and more generally, is the "equality" at issue strict equality, equality of

[2] Ryan, *Distributive Justice* (3rd edn.), pp. 180–181: "According to the rule of arithmetical equality, all persons who contribute to the product should receive the same amount of remuneration. With the exception of Bernard Shaw, no important writer defends this rule to-day. It is unjust because it would treat unequals equally. Although men are equal as moral entities, as human persons, they are unequal in desires, capacities, and powers. An income that would fully satisfy the needs of one man would meet only 75 per cent., or 50 per cent., of the capacities of another. To allot them equal amounts of income would be to treat them unequally with regard to the requisites of life and self development. To treat them unequally in these matters would be to treat them unequally as regards the real and only purpose of property rights. That purpose is welfare. Hence the equal moral claims of men which admittedly arise out of their moral equality must be construed as claims to equal degrees of welfare, not to equal amounts of external goods . . . Moreover, the rule of equal incomes is socially impracticable. It would deter the great majority of the more efficient from putting forth their best efforts and turning out their maximum product. As a consequence, the total volume of product would be so diminished as to render the share of the great majority of persons smaller than it would have been under a rational plan of unequal distribution."

sacrifice, equality of opportunity-and-risk, equality of rights, or equality of "consideration," etc.? [3]

A rule of strict equality violates the most elemental requisites of the concept of justice itself: justice not only requires the equal treatment of equals, as the canon at issue would certainly assure, but also under various circumstances requires the converse, the (appropriately measured) unequal treatment of unequals, a requisite which the canon violates blatantly. In any distribution among individuals whose legitimate claims with respect to this distribution are diverse, the treatment of people as equals without reference to their differential claims outrages rather than implements our sense of justice.

3. The Canon of Need

This canon holds that justice consists in the treatment of people according to their needs. Here we have the *socialistic* principle of the idealistic socialistic and communist theoreticians: "to each according to his needs." [4] Basically this principle is closely allied with the preceding one, and is, like it, one of *rectification*: recognizing that as things stand, men come into the world with different possessions and opportunities as well as differences in natural endowments, the principle professes to treat them, not equally, but so as to *make* them as equal as possible.

Regarding this principle, it has been said:

> If the task of distribution were entirely independent of the process of production, this rule would be ideal [from the stand-

[3] Regarding these problems, see S. I. Benn and R. S. Peters, *Social Principles and the Democratic State* (London: Allen & Unwin, 1959), ch. 5, "Justice and Equality."

[4] The formula "From each according to his abilities; to each according to his needs" was first advanced by the early French socialists of the Utopian school, and was officially adopted by German socialists in the Gotha Program of 1875.

> point of justice]; for it would treat men as equal in those
> respects in which they are equal; namely as beings endowed
> with the dignity and the potencies of personality; and it
> would treat them as unequal in those respects in which they are
> unequal; that is, in their desires and capacities.[5]

This limitation of the rule is of itself too narrow. The principle does recognize inequalities, but it recognizes only one sort; it rides roughshod not only over the matter of productive contributions but over all other ways of grounding legitimate claims (e.g., those based on kinship, on [nonproductive] services rendered, on contracts and compacts, etc.) that make for relevant differences, i.e., inequalities, among the potential recipients of a distribution. Nor, for that matter, is the principle as clear-cut as it seems on first view: by the time anything like an adequate analysis of "need" has been provided, the principle covers a wide-ranging area.[6] For example, are we to interpret the "needs" at issue as *real* needs or as *felt* needs?

4. The Canon of Ability and / or Achievement

This canon holds that justice consists in the treatment of people according to their abilities. Here we have the *meritarian* criterion going back to Aristotle and echoed by the (Jeffersonian) theorists of a "natural aristocracy of ability." Natural ability, however, is a latent quality which subsists in the mode of potentiality. It represents natural endowments that can be cultivated to varying degrees and may or may not become operative and actually put to work. To allocate rewards with reference solely to innate ability, unqualified by

[5] Ryan, *Distributive Justice* (3rd edn.), p. 181.
[6] See Benn and Peters, *Social Principles and the Democratic State*, pp. 141–148.

considerations of how the abilities in question are used or abused, would be to act in a way that is patently unjust. Moreover, a question can validly be raised as to the propriety of having natural ability—which is, after all, wholly a "gift of the gods" and in no way a matter of desert—count as the sole or even the primary basis of claims.[7]

This objection might be countered by granting that it may hold for *natural* (or innate) ability, but that it fails to be applicable when the "ability" at issue is an *acquired* ability, or perhaps even more aptly, a *demonstrated* ability of the persons at issue, as determined by their achievements. This is the criterion naturally used in giving grades to students and prizes to tennis players (where need, for instance, and effort are deliberately discounted). But in this case the canon becomes transformed, in its essentials, into the Canon of Productivity, which will be dealt with below.

5. *The Canon of Effort*

This canon holds that justice consists in the treatment of people according to their efforts and sacrifices on their own behalves, or perhaps on behalf of their group (family, society, fellowmen). Here we have the *puritanical* principle espoused by theorists of a "Puritan ethic," who hold that God helps (and men should help) those who help themselves. Burke lauded the "natural society" in which "it is an invariable law that a man's acquisitions are in proportion to his labors."[8]

---

7 "That part of a man's income which he owes to the possession of extra-ordinary natural abilities is a free boon to him; and from an abstract point of view bears some resemblance to the rent of other free gifts of nature. . . ." A. Marshall, *Principles of Economics* (8th edn., London: Macmillan, 1920), p. 664. The receipt of such "rents" is surely a matter of capitalizing on public necessity rather than one of obtaining the just reward due to individual desert.

8 Edmund Burke, *Vindication of a Natural Society*, cited by E. Halévy in *The Growth of Philosophic Radicalism*, tr. Mary Morris, p. 216.

Think also of the historic discussions of a just wage and the traditional justification of differential wage scales. On the question of wages, classical socialists such as Fourier and St. Simon argued that the wage should be inversely proportioned to the intrinsic pleasantness (interest, appeal, prestige) of the task. (Presumably, thus, the policeman walking the beat shall receive more than the captain sitting at headquarters.) But the difficulties of this standpoint lie on the surface, e.g., the difficulty of maintaining morale and discipline in a setting in which the claims of ability and responsibility go unrecognized.

Moreover, the principle ignores the fact that effort is of its very nature a many-sided thing: it can be either fruitful or vain, well-directed or misguided, properly applied or misapplied, availing or unavailing, etc. To allocate rewards by effort as such without reference to its nature and direction is to ignore a key facet of just procedure—to fail to make a distinction that makes a difference. Also, to reward by effort rather than achievement is socially undesirable: it weakens incentive and encourages the inefficient, the untalented, the incompetent.

6. *The Canon of Productivity*

This canon holds that justice consists in the treatment of people according to their actual productive contribution to their group.[9] Here we have the essentially economic principle of the social-welfare-minded *capitalistic* theoreticians. The claim-bases at issue here are primarily those traditionally considered in economics: services rendered, capital advanced, risks run, and the like. Much is to be said on behalf of this principle as a *restricted* rule, governing the division of proceeds and profits resulting from a common productive enterprise;

---

[9] Two alternative constructions of the principle arise, according as the "productive contribution" at issue is construed as the *total* contribution, or as solely the *net* contribution, i.e., the part that is available for consumption by others after deletion of the producers' own share.

but it is clearly defective as a general principle of distributive justice, simply because it is an overly limited single-factor criterion. The principle is prepared to put aside all considerations not only of unmerited claims in general, but also of merited claims when merited through extra-productive factors such as need and effort.

Yet one cannot fail to be impressed by the appeal to justice of such an argument as the following:

> When men of equal productive power are performing the same kind of labour, superior amounts of product do represent superior amounts of effort. . . . If men are unequal in productive power their products are obviously not in proportion to their efforts. Consider two men whose natural physical abilities are so unequal that they can handle with equal effort shovels differing in capacity by fifty per cent. Instances of this kind are innumerable in industry. If these two men are rewarded according to productivity, one will get fifty per cent more compensation than the other. Yet the surplus received by the more fortunate man does not represent any action or quality for which he is personally responsible. It corresponds to no larger output of personal effort, no superior exercise of will, no greater personal desert.[10]

Note here the criticism of a (restricted) purely economic application of the principle by an appeal to one's sense of justice. If such an appeal is to be given but the slightest (even if not ultimately decisive) weight, as I think it must, then the canon in question must *a fortiori* be at once abandoned as an exclusive and exhaustive general principle of distributive justice.

7. The Canon of Social Utility

This canon holds that justice consists in the treatment of people according to the best prospects for advancing the com-

10 Ryan, *Distributive Justice* (3rd edn.), pp. 183–184.

mon good, or the public interest, or the welfare of mankind, or the greater good of a greater number. The theory has two basic variants, according as one resorts to a distinction between the common good of men considered *collectively*, as constituting a social group with some sort of life of its own, or merely *distributively*, as an aggregation of separate individuals. In the former case we have the "public interest," expedientialist variant of the canon with roots going back to Hebraic theology, Stoic philosophy, and Roman jurisprudence (*pro bono publico*). In the second case we have the *utilitarian* and more modern, individualistic version of the canon.

The same fundamental criticism (already dwelt upon at considerable length in our preceding discussion) can be deployed against both versions of the theory: an individual's *proper share viewed from the angle of the general good* cannot be equated with his *just share* pure and simple, because there is no "pre-established harmony" to guarantee that all of the individual's legitimate claims (the authoritative determinants of his just share) be recognized and acceded to when "the *general* good" becomes the decisive criterion. And insofar as these legitimate claims are disallowed—or *could* be disallowed —in a patently unjust (though socially advantageous) way, the principle of the primacy of the general good exhibits a feature which precludes its acceptance as a principle of justice.

8. *The Canon of Supply and Demand*

This canon holds that justice consists in the treatment of people according to a valuation of their socially useful—or perhaps merely desired—contributions, these being evaluated not on the basis of the value of the product (as with the Canon of Productivity above), but on the basis of relative scarcity of the service. Here we have the essentially economic principle of the more hard-boiled "play of the market" school of laissez-faire theoreticians. The train dispatcher would thus deserve a larger part of the proceeds of the joint operation than the conductor, the general manager more than the section foreman, the buyer more than the salesgirl, because—while in each case both kinds of contribution are alike essential to the enterprise—the former type of labor calls for skills that are relatively scarcer, being less plentifully diffused throughout the working population. Such valuation then rests not upon the relative extent or intrinsic merit of the contribution made, but upon the fact that that contribution is viewed by the community as necessary or desirable, and can either be made successfully by fewer people, or else involves such expenditures, risks, hardships, or hazards that fewer people are willing to undertake the task. (Throughout recent years successful entertainers have been remunerated more highly than successful physicians—and on this principle, justly so.)

As a criterion of justice, this canon suffers from the same general defects as does the Canon of Productivity which it seeks to qualify. Not only does it put aside any accommodation of unmerited claims, but also any claims based upon factors (such as individual need and expenditure of effort) which have no basis in the making of a productive contribution to felt social needs.

9. Our Own Position: The Canon of Claims

One and the same shortcoming runs through all of the above canons of distributive justice: they are all *monistic*. They all recognize but one solitary, homogeneous mode of claim production (be it need, effort, productivity, or whatever), to the exclusion of all others. A single specific ground of claim establishment is canonized as uniquely authoritative, and all the others dismissed. As a result, these canons all suffer the aristocratic fault of hyperexclusiveness. As we see it, they err not so much in commission as in omission.

To correct this failing requires that we go from a concept of claim establishment that is monistic and homogeneous to one that is pluralistic and heterogeneous. To do so we put forward, as representing (in essentials) our own position on the issue of distributive justice, the CANON OF CLAIMS: Distributive justice consists in the treatment of people *according to their legitimate claims,* positive and negative. This canon shifts the burden to—and thus its implementation hinges crucially upon—the question of the nature of legitimate claims, and of the machinery for their mutual accommodation in cases of plurality, and their reconciliation in cases of conflict. To say this is not a criticism of the principle, but simply the recognition of an inevitable difficulty which must be encountered by any theory of distributive justice at the penalty of showing itself grossly inadequate.

The Canon of Claims plainly avoids the fault of overrestrictiveness: indeed, it reaches out to embrace all the other canons. From its perspective each canon represents one particular sort of ground (need, effort, productivity, etc.) on whose basis certain legitimate claims—upon whose accommodation it insists—can be advanced. The evaluation of these claims in context, and their due recognition under the circumstances, is in our view the key element of distributive justice.

We must be prepared to take such a multifaceted approach to claims because of the propriety of recognizing different kinds of claim-grounds as appropriate types of distribution. Our society inclines to the view that in the case of wages, desert is to be measured according to productivity of contribution qualified by supply-and-demand considerations; in the case of property income, by productivity considerations; in public-welfare distributions, by need qualified to avoid the demoralization inherent in certain types of means-tests; and in the negative distributions of taxation, by ability-to-pay qualified by social-utility considerations. The list could be extended and refined at great length but is already extensive enough to lend support to our pluralistic view of claims.

One important consequence of our canon must be noted. With it, the concept of justice is no solitarily self-sufficient ultimate, but becomes dependent upon the articulation of certain coordinate ideas, namely, those relating to claims and their establishment. The unraveling of the short thesis that distributive justice requires (in general) the accommodation of legitimate claims is but the preface of a long story about claims, a story for which there is neither need nor space here. Moreover, since claims themselves are not (at any rate, not in general) established by considerations of abstract justice, but are in large part grounded in positive law, the heavy dependence of justice upon a body of positive law may be seen. Where abstract justice might countenance various alternative divisions, the law specifies one particular procedure that underwrites a certain specific set of claims. That law shall embody considerations of justice is a trite thesis, but that there is a converse requirement resulting in mutual dependence is less frequently observed.

In espousing the Canon of Claims we may note that the search for a canon of distributive justice is carried back to the Roman jurists' view that the definitive principle of justice is inherent in the dictum *suum cuique tribuens*—"giving each his own." To the question *What is his own?* we have given the answer *What he deserves!* that is, a share ideally equal—or at any rate generally proportional—to his legitimate claims.

We must, however, be prepared to recognize that this principle of distributive justice needs some important qualifications. These qualifications involve difficulties of such magnitude for the theory of distributive justice that they must be dealt with in a separate chapter.

5

Complications
Affecting the
Justice of
Distributions

---

1. Facets of a Distribution

There are several distinct facets of distribution of which an adequate theory of distributive justice must be prepared to take account. The most important of these are the following three:

1) The total *amount of goods* (or utility) to be distributed,
2) The *pattern of distribution* arrived at, and
3) The *distributing procedure*, that is, the principle of selection by means of which the distribution is arrived at.

Item (2) has already been given prolonged attention, and we propose to return to (1) at some length in the next section, but (3) requires our present attention. The fact is that a distributing procedure can be more or less just (equitable, fair, reasonable), exactly as a distribution itself can be. To show this, it suffices to consider a choice between two alternative patterns of distribution, one of them grossly unjust, the other perfectly just. Assume now that the choice between these two alternative distribution schemes is *made by the toss of a coin.* Even if it turns out that the distribution ultimately arrived at is the proper one, one cannot say that the interests of distributive justice have been served adequately. (Just as the interests of punitive justice are not served by a procedure that cannot be relied upon to lead to a correct result, but may conceivably do so, such as a trial by lottery or combat, even when this so eventuates that "things come out all right.") As is generally the case, account must be taken not only of the result but of the procedures by which it is attained. John Hospers has stated the point well:

> We are concerned here [in the analysis of distributive justice] with which an ideal system of material rewards *would be,* not with how they *should be* brought about. If they were brought about by force, whim, or the arbitrary fiat of the bureaucrats on a regulatory commission, the results would probably be worse than that of the most flagrant injustices created without such fiat.[1]

The question of the acceptability of distributing procedures becomes particularly acute in the case of redistribution. Suppose that a certain body of goods (say, 6 units) is to be divided among Messrs A, B, and C, all of whom have equal claims. The resulting distribution of shares (a), (b), and (c), respectively, should of course be:

Share	Units
(a)	2
(b)	2
(c)	2

But suppose that the distribution has already been made—somehow, but not by A's or C's doings—as follows:

Share	Units
(a)	3
(b)	2
(c)	1

At this historic juncture we cannot simply redistribute back to the initial scheme and look on the whole transaction as but a single, complex two-stage distribution procedure. This is so

[1] *Human Conduct,* p. 434 n.

because once the initial distribution has actually gone into effect, new claims spring into being which cannot in justice be ignored. However, the topic of redistribution is a large one in its own right, and we cannot do more here than note its existence and recognize its difficulties.[2]

We must distinguish, then, between the merit of distributions on the one hand and that of distributing procedures on the other. Our ideal should of course be "just distributions justly arrived at." But we must be prepared for the sad recognition that here, as elsewhere, circumstances can arise in which the ideal is unattainable. Certain categories of "difficult situations" arise in special circumstances—in the case of indivisible (unsharable) goods, for example, or in that of an economy of scarcity—posing situations in which this ideal is in principle unattainable, and therefore cannot here reasonably be regarded as appropriate. The consideration of such special problems is the main task of the present chapter.

2. *The Role of Production*

Special heed must be given to item (1) in the list above: the *total amount* of goods (or utility) to be distributed. That explicit recognition is given to this factor both in the principle of utility's insistence upon "the *greatest* good" and in the Marxist dictum *"From each according to ability!"* must be regarded as points in their favor. Any theory of distributive justice that fails to make provision for a *principle of production* of goods and merely insists upon the fairness and equity of distribution of such goods as lie at hand is gravely deficient, because the very notion of justice itself, as we shall argue, alters its workings with the special circumstances—such as those of indivisible goods, of an economy of scarcity, and of an economy of abundance.

The role of production can be illustrated graphically by

2 See B. de Jouvenel, *The Ethics of Redistribution.*

citing a passage from John A. Ryan's *Distributive Justice,* written some fifty years ago:

> No conceivable method of distributing the present national product would provide every family with the means of supporting an automobile, or any equivalent symbol of comfort. Indeed, there are indications that the present amount of product per capita cannot long be maintained without . . . vastly greater efficiency on the part of both capital and labour.[3]

The sought-for "vastly greater efficiency" has been achieved in the United States economy doubtless to an extent greatly beyond Ryan's most hopeful dreams; and with it, important problems of distributive justice (e.g., who are to be the happy few enjoying that "symbol of comfort," the automobile) have altogether vanished. Production plays a crucial role in the theory of distributive justice because the problem of just distribution is less urgent for an abundant good and simply *does not arise* with a genuinely superabundant good (e.g., air for breathing in the country—though not necessarily in the modern city, alas). Where each has "all he wants," the question of the *pattern of distribution* sinks into irrelevance.

3. Justice in the Narrower and the Wider Senses

The central and most crucially important contention of this chapter, perhaps of the book, is that there are two distinct senses of *justice,* corresponding to two diverse articulations of the concept itself. There is *justice in the narrower sense of fairness,* on the one hand, and on the other, *justice in a wider sense, taking account of the general good.* These two types of justice are distinct, and can even come into conflict with one another.

[3] Ryan, *Distributive Justice* (1st edn., 1916), p. 432.

The position we wish to adopt was adumbrated—to be sure with a different application in mind—by the judicious Sidgwick:

> It may be said that the notion of Fairness and Equity which we ordinarily apply . . . is to be distinguished from that of Justice; Equity being in fact often contrasted with strict Justice, and conceived as capable of coming into collision with it. And this is partly true; but I think the wider and no less usual sense of the term Justice, in which it includes Equity or Fairness, is the only one that can be conveniently adopted in an ethical treatise. . . .[4]

The possibility of conflict between fairness and justice in the wider sense can be seen in a simple example. Suppose that Messrs A, B, and C (assumed to be equal in point of merit) were to get the utility shares (a), (b), and (c), respectively, in accord with one of the two schemes:

SCHEME I   SCHEME II

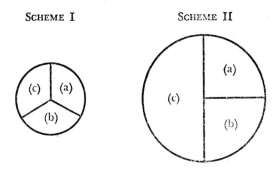

Patently Scheme I effects the fairer (indeed a perfectly fair) distribution. From the standpoint of "justice in the narrower sense" it has the clear-cut advantage. But that Scheme II is

4 Sidgwick, *The Methods of Ethics* pp. 284–285. Sidgwick's use for the distinction between justice and fairness is, however, quite different from ours. For a view contrary to both positions see John Rawls, "Justice as Fairness," *The Philosophical Review*, LXVII (1958), 164–194. Sidgwick wants to regard fairness as a subordinate component of justice, as do we ourselves; whereas Rawls treats fairness as the more fundamental conception.

superior from the standpoint of the interests of all concerned is equally clear: everyone would be the gainer by its adoption. Despite its lesser *fairness*, the advantage from the standpoint of "justice in the wider sense" lies with this scheme. An arbiter who opts for Scheme II is surely more just (and in no case any less just) than his incontestably fairer counterpart who opts for Scheme I. "Not fair but just" has the air of a paradox, perhaps, but it is not a contradiction in terms. For fairness is just *fairness*, period; but justice in its fullest extension requires that account be taken also of the common good (the general advantage, the general interest). Embracing a "principle of production" of the type described in the preceding section, the conception of Justice in this full-blooded sense incorporates recognition of the fact that an adequate theory for the evaluation of distributions cannot confine its attention to fairness alone.

A perhaps unpleasant but nonetheless important insight is the recognition that some of Western man's most treasured values stand in dynamic tension with one another. A significant instance is the mutual tension between freedom and equality in the social and economic sphere: unrestricted freedom of action is likely to result in inequalities; undiluted equality cannot be realized without serious restrictions upon freedom.[5] In an analogous way, the realization of Justice with a capital J requires the fusion of considerations of utility and the common good with those of justice in the narrower, restricted sense of fairness. True justice is neither to be determined by considerations of fairness and equity alone, or without any reference to considerations of fairness and equity alone, or without any reference to considerations of social advantage; nor is its ultimate arbiter the general good alone without reference to claims, rights, and desert: its determination requires the appropriate conjoint *coordination* of these

[5] For an interesting development of this thesis see G. Dietze, *In Defense of Property* (Chicago: Henry Regnery, 1963).

two at-times-divergent factors. (Justice, in both the wider and narrower senses we have defined, abstracts from those individual choices in which "more than justice" is involved. The man who *deliberately* chooses to take less than his share creates a situation that is non-just, though certainly not to be condemned as unjust.)

The preceding example drives home the critical importance of a Principle of Production for the theory of distributive justice. If we are willing—as I think we must be—to permit considerations of justice in the narrower sense of fairness to be *overshadowed* by considerations of justice in a wider sense that takes into account the common good, then we have to be prepared to recognize the superiority of "unfair" distributions whose unfairness "pays for itself" by bringing greater advantage to all. We may well be prepared to tolerate discrepancies in the fairness of a distribution in contexts where these *could only be removed by exacting an unreasonable price* from all or most or the least well-off of the individuals involved; but how can the unfair possibly be condemned as unjust in a situation where its presence represents a social advantage profiting all? (This insight catches one of the strengths of the principle of utility.) It is unquestionably the case that justice in the narrower sense of fairness is an important element of Justice in the wider sense, but it is here only one element among several others, among which "the general good" is the prominent if not predominant consideration.

4. *Indivisible Goods and "Equality of Opportunity"*

An important facet of the role of distributing *procedures* comes to the fore whenever in the nature of things a straightforwardly equitable pattern of distribution is impossible of realization. This occurs *inter alia* whenever the object of the division is an indivisible (or a not sufficiently divisible) good. It happens, for example, when precedence must be given to one of two ambassadors whose claims are perfectly equal. Here it is *in principle impossible* for the "ultimate distribution of utility" that is actually arrived at to be "fairly divided" in a strict sense (i.e., divided in rigid correspondence with what we have called the "proportionality principle" of adjusting shares to the strength of the claims of the respective claimants). The interests of "distributive justice" cannot here—in the very nature of the case—be served by dividing the utility, but only by resorting to a stochastic method for dividing the "expected utility," by equalizing the *chances* of the equally matched claimants to carry off the whole of the indivisible prize. This random-distribution method is in fact the standard procedure in everyday life when such problems arise, e.g., a coin is tossed in cases like our precedence example.

A consideration of the issues posed for the theory of distributive justice by the problem of indivisible goods points to an important result. A distribution that does not give all equally deserving claimants an equal share must, in the interests of justice, at least preserve an "equality of opportunity" (and, of course, one of risk also). In this way the element of fairness (and thus of justice) can be introduced into situations in which straightforwardly fair distributions—the ideal of distributive justice—lie outside the realizable practicalities.

It should, however, be noted that this resort to the concept of "equality of opportunity" is a *faute de mieux* procedure, a counsel of despair, as it were. It represents a means for achieving an equalization of opportunities (and risks) in cases in which a direct allocation of shares to claims is infeasible. A good example is provided by automobile traffic in modern America, an economically and socially advantageous institution inflicting gross damage (both physical and monetary) on the thousands of people involved in accidents every year.

There is no way of dividing the damage equally among those who benefit from the use of motor vehicles. The best that can be done is to equalize as much as possible the damage and the loss through some such measure as legally mandatory liability insurance.

5. *Special Problems of an Economy of Scarcity*

We have been distinguishing between the narrower sense of distributive justice as fairness in the allocation of shares and a wider sense in which considerations of "the general good" are also allowed to play a role. In insisting that the interests of distributive justice are not served by considerations of fairness alone we subscribe to a dictum that may sound harsh, but it is true nonetheless. Consider a drastic case of an "economy of scarcity," e.g., one with three people (whose claims are equal) and a total amount of utility which is so small that when it is divided equitably everyone is put below the level of minimal adequacy (see Chapter Two, pp. 28–30). Contrast two modes of distribution (with 1 as the acceptably minimal "floor"):

Share	SCHEME I	SCHEME II
(a)	0.7 units	1 unit
(b)	0.7	1
(c)	0.7	0.1

Scheme I puts everyone at the same *ex hypothesi* sub-minimal level. Although it answers to the "principle of justice" (share received proportional to desert), it has the disadvantage of maximizing the number of persons in a state of utility deprivation. Scheme II puts the recipients of shares (a) and (b) above, i.e., *just* above the minimal level, leaving the (insufficient) rest for the recipient of (c). Which scheme of distribution better serves the interests of distributive justice? Scheme I is obviously the fairer. Scheme II however has much to be said on its behalf: recognizing the inadequacy of goods, it puts as many as possible of the persons involved on a level above the minimal tolerance level.

Of course adoption of Scheme II would have to be implemented by assigning the recipient of (c) by some lottery procedure (our operating assumptions preclude the enlistment of volunteers). In failing to equalize the shares it should at least be assured that all concerned should have an equal chance of obtaining a satisfactory lot. Again, "equality of opportunity" —or rather, here, "equality of risk"—provides a means of quasi-equalization in a situation in which equalization pure and simple is infeasible, or rather, is undesirable.

The example of such an economy of scarcity again shows that from the angle of distributive justice the *fairness* of a distribution can be a consideration secondary to that of the *total* at issue: the question of fairness can become irrelevant when the entire amount is too small.[6]

An *economy of scarcity* is, by definition, one in which justice (in a restricted sense of the term) cannot be done, because there is not "enough to go around": if everyone is given a "share proportional to his claims and desert" then someone— or everyone—is pressed beneath the floor of the minimally acceptable level. Actually, it would be appropriate to distinguish between (1) an economy of scarcity that is one of *mere insufficiency,* in that while there is not enough to satisfy everyone's legitimate claims, implementation of the "claims-proportionate-to-desert" principle does not push anyone beneath the

[6] A recent work stressing the importance for moral philosophy of the economic concept of scarcity is V. C. Walsh's *Scarcity and Evil* (Englewood Cliffs, N. J.: Prentice-Hall, 1951). Here, however, the implications of scarcity are explored from the standpoint of individual morality, rather than from the social standpoint, and scarcity is treated in the context of guilt and responsibility rather than—as with our present discussion—in the context of justice.

floor of the acceptable minimum; and (2) an economy of scarcity that is one of *dire insufficiency,* in that it is such as to require abandonment of the proportionality rule if the catastrophe-prevention principle is accepted. Asked to attain strict justice in a case of this sort, we must offer the now nonparadoxical reply that "one can't get there from here." In this context, the interests of justice can only be served by *avoidance.*

It seems a plausible contention that entirely different principles of distribution should prevail in an economy of scarcity and in an economy of sufficiency. In the latter a policy of "shares proportioned to desert" can be applied without qualification. But in the former it seems a not merely *expedient* but even (in the wider sense) a just rule—one best serving the aim of effecting justice in the circumstances—that: *The number of individuals whose share of utility falls below the "minimal" level is to be made as small as possible.* To this overriding principle even considerations of equity (fairness) should be made to give way. In an economy of simple sufficiency, on the other hand, the narrower principle of distributive justice as equity should be allowed to hold undisturbed sway.

An example may help to motivate such a recourse to the concept of a *utility floor.* Consider the following problem of dividing a good of limited divisibility in an economy of scarcity: Suppose five marbles are to be divided among five boys, four of whom (boys *A* to *D*) are equally deserving (from the angle of the considerations relevant here), the remaining one *(E)* being exactly twice as deserving as any of the rest. Consider now a choice between the following divisions:

SCHEME I		SCHEME II	
A	⎫ 1 marble	A	1 marble
B	⎬ apiece for all but one	B	1
C	⎪ (selected at random)	C	1
D	⎭	D	1
E	2 marbles	E	1

One feels instinctively (I believe) that Scheme II is preferable to Scheme I. This is so, not because the first scheme is any less satisfactory as a procedure for aligning the distribution of goods with the desert of the recipients, but because the second scheme prevents anyone falling into the state of "utility deprivation" for whose avoidance the idea of a utility floor was initially introduced.

6. *Special Problems of an Economy of Abundance*

We have to this point distinguished between a utility economy that is an economy of scarcity and one that is an economy of sufficiency. And we have seen that this distinction is crucial for the issue of distributive justice, because quite different principles apply in the two cases—minimization of "utility deprivation" on the one hand and equalization of shares to claims on the other. The thesis of the present section is that yet further complications must be introduced to deal adequately with the case of an "economy of abundance."

Consider again for a moment the idea of a minimum level of utility, the *utility floor* that played so central a role in our analysis of justice in an economy of scarcity. But how was the idea of a minimum level to be understood? Clearly in terms of bare biologico-physical survival. Think, for example, of the traditional concept of a "living wage," with "living" to be understood as *just* living: recall the frequent references to subsistence levels and "starvation limits" in the older economic literature. In the eighteenth century it was axiomatic to say of the common workman that, in Turgot's words, *Il ne gagne que sa vie.*

In an economy of abundance it becomes not only possible but plausible, and indeed at a certain point imperative, to elevate one's conception of a minimally tolerable share of utility. The fact that as a utility economy rises from a condition of scarcity to one of sufficiency to one of abundance the escalation of the minimal level inevitably becomes warranted, is of crucial importance for the theory of distributive justice. The minimum is raised from *bare survival* to *at-least-modestly-pleasant survival* to *a share in the good life*. As society—and the economy that is its productive sector—becomes able to "afford" more and more in the passage from adequacy to abundance, an elevation in the level of expectation of its members becomes inevitable, and our levels of "tolerable minimality" are revised drastically upward.[7]

The upshot of this phenomenon is a seemingly paradoxical result: We find ourselves once more in the situation of an economy of scarcity—or perhaps we should, to avoid confusion, call it an "economy of felt insufficiency." The economy is not, strictly speaking, one of scarcity, but "for practical purposes" treated as such. Once more the guiding principle of distributive justice is the minimization of persons in a state of utility deprivation, with "deprivation" now understood in a revised and metaphorical sense. In such a situation of minima based not on real scarcity but on "felt insufficiency," we have to do with "minima" not in the absolute sense of biologico-physical survival, but rather in the form of a relative, sliding-scale conception of "a satisfactory life."

At this point the theory of distributive justice joins frontiers with the wider notion of socio-economic justice based on the idea of "what the society can afford." It is here that the abstract idea of a reasonable "escalation of minima" receives its operative impetus.

---

[7] Thomas Paine proposed in 1797 that England establish a national fund from which everyone should receive £15 at age 21 and £10 at age 50 "to enable them to live without wretchedness and to go decently out of the world." Contrast with this modest provision the far-reaching arrangements of the modern welfare state, sometimes so grandiose that it can be questioned (e.g., in regard to England) whether the society can in fact afford to meet the level of expectation that is being set.

An illustration of the actual workings of this reasoning is the current, more and more frequently voiced doctrine of a basic "living allotment" for every American, by means of some such device as negative income taxation. In the old conception of the matter by liberal economic theoreticians, the society and its economy owed to every one of its *working participants* a "living wage" (certainly for himself, and perhaps also for some average number of dependents). Because our economy has grown increasingly affluent, there is now widespread concern that the society and its economy owes to every one of its *members* a "living wage," irrespective of any productive contribution. (In an economy of overproduction, there is something to be said for the creation not of incentives to produce, i.e., to participate in the economy as a net contributor, but of incentives to consume, i.e., to participate as a net drain, and to provide a motivation not for productive work but for constructive idleness.) The practice of Keynesian economics has already brought us a long way down the road of this conception. At present (1965) wage levels something like 4.5–5% of those able to work (predominantly in the category of unskilled labor) are unemployed. A downward shift in the wage rate *of the entire unskilled group* could result in the absorption of the greater part of this 4.5–5% in the work force. But rather than lower the standard of many to raise that of some, the society chooses to tolerate this level of unemployment, taxing the employed to provide various types of social-insurance compensation for the unemployed.[8]

Moreover, in our economy of abundance the very terms of

[8] There is, however, no gainsaying the fact that this one-sidedly economic approach to the problem slurs over an important aspect of human psychology: the deep-rooted yearning of many or most men to make some positive contribution to the welfare of their group, and to have some task entitling them to the respect that their fellows accord those participating in the world's work. Economic measures that promote unemployment exact from the unemployed not only a loss of wages, which it may be easy to make up, but a sacrifice in self-respect and social respect which is not so readily compensable under currently existing conditions.

reference in such discussions have undergone a qualitative change, because the economists' concept of a "living wage" has undergone substantial escalation. For example, their concept now includes not only the minimalities of food, clothing, and shelter—in respect to each of which there has also been escalation—but also entirely new means for protections against the normal hazards of life, e.g., insurance against illness and accidents. The "living" at issue here is no longer to be taken as *mere* living, as bare survival, but is to be construed in terms of some measure of "the good life." The idea of a living wage has become tied to our concept of a rising standard of living and has, in consequence, undergone substantial escalation. It is this fact that—somewhat paradoxically—renders our affluent society an "economy of scarcity" in a very real and significant respect: the idea of "catastrophe prevention" is again operative, but now with a very altered notion of a "catastrophe." [9]

7. Justice and Inequality

There is an aspect of an economy of more-than-sufficiency (abundance) that bears importantly on the question of the justice of distributions in that it can serve under special circumstances to abrogate applicability of the "claims proportionate to desert" principle. Such inequalities in a distribution are compatible with distributive justice when they "pay for themselves," as it were, in terms of conducing to the gen-

---

[9] "Between 1914 and 1937 average real earnings in the United Kingdom increased by approximately one-third. Resentment against the co-existence of needless disabilities and preferential advantages was not weakened by that upward movement, but strengthened by it" (R. H. Tawney, *Equality*, 4th edn., p. 255). No doubt this reaction is in part stimulated by the fact that whereas an affluent society can afford the path of social improvement, it tends in large measure to follow that of wastefulness and inefficiency in production and social noxiousness in consumption. (It is clearly debatable, however, whether the redeployment of resources from the private to the public sector is the best way to skin this particular cat.)

eral good. It was, in fact, this line of thought that lay behind the conception of an effective average as introduced in Chapter Two. For one of the guiding ideas of this conception is that in certain cases one can "pay the price" for tolerating inequalities in terms of a compensating increase in the general good. A perfectly acceptable distribution gives *A* a larger share than the equally deserving *B* in a distribution scheme which gives everyone, including *B*, a larger share than he would obtain on the alternative distribution schemes. It is, to be sure, *unfair* that *A* shall fare better than *B*, but it is not *unjust*, for (1) it is not the case that *A*'s improved position is obtained *at the expense* of *B*, and (2) the unfairness at issue could not (*ex hypothesi*) be removed without damaging all the interests at issue. Crudely put, the case is one in which it is rational to subordinate envy to cupidity—it would be wholly indefensible for us (or even for *B* himself) to deny *B* some benefit to prevent an even larger benefit from accruing to *A*.

The tables are now turned regarding our earlier criticism of utilitarianism's narrow focus upon the general good to the exclusion of considerations of justice. For a narrow-minded insistence upon justice (in the restricted sense of fairness of equity) at all costs commits exactly the opposite fallacy. In brushing aside considerations of general advantage, the *fiat justitia ruat caelum* school of thought becomes objectionable at the opposite extreme. Our thesis is that justice (in the narrow sense) and the general good of utilitarianism must be *coordinated* with one another, and that just this constitutes Justice in its wider sense.

This brings us to the classic and, so far as I know, never successfully rebutted defense of inequality in the economic sphere. What is at issue is the matter of *incentives* needed to induce the employment of talents and skills in limited supply in socially desirable directions (desirable innovation, appropriate risk-taking, development of human resources, economic growth, etc.). The justification for the allocation of an enlarged share of goods to an individual does not now hinge upon anything that could legitimately be regarded as purely and wholly a *claim* of his, but is determined rather by the interests and felt needs of the society. It is not that the individual at issue has a somehow amplified claim upon the product of the society that is eager to enlist his services: he is to receive more not because he *deserves* to have an augmented share but because it is *expedient* to give it to him in the interests of the general welfare (for instance, because a greater total body of goods results which ultimately redounds to everyone's advantage, including that of the "short-time losers" whose shares were diminished because of the augmented share in question; or perhaps it redounds to the advantage not of the then-and-there members of society but of their posterity).[10]

An appeal to incentives, although the major line of social-utility defense of economic inequalities, is not the only one. Another important example is the traditional rationalization of male primogeniture under certain circumstances (say, when it preserves the economic viability of an agrarian system).[11] On this line of defense, certain sorts of inequalities can indeed be justified, but only when they are "paid for" in terms of social advantage. Beginning at an egalitarian starting point, economic inequalities or the social inequalities that go with

---

10 "How can we justify the superior rewards of that scarcity which is not due to unusual costs of any sort, but merely to restricted opportunity? So far as society is concerned, the answer is simple: the practice pays. As to the possessors of the rarer kinds of ability, they are in about the same ethical position as those persons whose superior productivity is derived entirely from superior native endowment. In both cases the unusual rewards are due to factors outside the control of the recipients; to advantages which they themselves have not brought into existence. In the former case the decisive factor and advantage is opportunity; in the latter it is a gift of the Creator." Ryan, *Distributive Justice* (3rd edn.), p. 187.
11 See T. N. Carver, *Essays in Social Justice* (Cambridge: Harvard University Press, 1915), pp. 292–293.

differences in rank and office are defensible when they in fact conduce to the success of the enterprise at issue and thence to the general advantage.[12] To take this view is to accept the position that, under restricted circumstances, it is defensible to sacrifice justice (i.e., equity) to the general interest (public welfare, the standard of living). This resort to a utilitarian perspective is not a matter of a *callous disregard* of fairness and equity, but a *reluctant concession* that is made *faute de mieux* under the constraint of recalcitrant circumstance.[13]

In summary, then, the point is that such an allocation of shares in the social product, based not solely on the claims of individuals but also making certain (restricted) allowances for the general good and the "interests of society" (including its as yet inexistent posterity), can be regarded as justifiable. The resulting distribution will be a just one in exactly that wider sense of the term which, as we have argued above, must be distinguished from the narrower sense of distributive justice as fairness pure and simple.

8. The Complexity of the Evaluation of Distributions

A brief retrospect of our findings in the present chapter is in order. We have seen that the matter of a principle of distribu-

---

12 It deserves note, however, that the conception of "the public good," or "the interest of the community" at issue here, while prepared to depart from egalitarianism, does not abandon the radical individualism of the classical utilitarians (i.e., does not move in the direction of corporatism and *raison d'état*). For the position of the utilitarians see E. Halévy, *The Growth of Philosophic Radicalism*, tr. Mary Morris, pp. 499–503.

13 "Now inequalities of fortune—abstracted the cases of governor and general and every species of trustee for the advantage of others— are generally explained by utilitarians as the consequences of conventions clear and fixed for preventing confusion and encouraging production, but not otherwise desirable, or rather of which the necessity is regretted." F. Y. Edgeworth, *Mathematical Psychics*, p. 77.

tive justice is shot through with complications. In particular, the fundamental Canon of Claims ("Let the division be such that shares are proportioned to claims") is wholly unproblematic only in the case of a utility economy that is an economy of sufficiency, but needs to be circumscribed by a series of qualifications under other circumstances, as follows:

1) In a utility economy that is an economy of scarcity. Here the principle must be modified to allow a minimization—preserving "equality of opportunity," or rather of risk—of the number of persons involved who are put into a state of "utility deprivation" by receiving a subminimal share.

2) When "indivisible goods" are involved in the distribution in such a way that a proportioning of shares to claims may be impossible. This situation serves to create an artificial economy of scarcity. Here our principle must again be to do "the best we can" to achieve an ideal distribution, recognizing that the very closest we can come may be no further than an "equality of opportunity" leading to—and atoning for—a very unequal division of the goods divided.

3) In a utility economy that is an economy of abundance (or even of superabundance). Here the principle must be so modified as to implement a distinction between *justice* in the narrower sense of fairness and *Justice* in the wider sense of the general good. This works in at least three important ways: (a) when some seemingly unjust distribution works to everyone's advantage because the total to be distributed becomes relatively larger (this justifies, for example, the use of *incentives*); (b) when the "interests of society" apart from those of its present participants—namely, when the interests of posterity—are served by a prima facie unbalanced distribution; (c) when an "escalation of minima" ren-

ders the economy of abundance one which in an artificial sense *is* and in practice actually becomes treated as an economy of scarcity. (These points, especially the last, require further development, and we shall return to the issue in Section Ten below.)

This set of considerations makes it clear that the question of a Canon of Distributive Justice is not to be settled *in abstracto*, disregarding the sort of utility economy that is at issue. Whether this economy is one of scarcity, of sufficiency, or of abundance (or even superabundance), becomes a crucial issue that must be resolved first, before the preferability of alternative distributions can be settled by an invocation of principles. The characteristics of the economy of goods within which the distributions are supposed to take place represent crucially important contextual or environmental factors affecting the justice of distributions. Without careful heed of these factors, the relative merits of alternative distributions, from the standpoint of distributive justice, cannot be assessed in an appropriate and acceptable way.

9. Justice and Scarcity: Another Look at the Approach of Welfare Economics

In Chapter One modern welfare economics was criticized for its tendency to sidestep the problem of distribution. The time has come to qualify this criticism. To be sure, the reasons advanced by the economists in question to justify, for example, the Kaldor-Hicks Criterion strike us as grossly deficient. But all the same, the welfare economists' concentration upon production and de-emphasis of distribution can be provided with a rationale that is viable even from the angle of what on first view seems to be its weakest point—distributive justice.

The upshot of this chapter has been that the workings of the concept of distributive justice are a function of scarcity. In an *economy of scarcity,* seemingly inequitable distributions may be optimal; in an *economy of sufficiency* (i.e., bare sufficiency), we must of course strive for equity; in an *economy of abundance,* inequities may serve the cause of distributive justice when they "pay for themselves" in the appropriate way; and, finally, in an *economy of superabundance* where everyone has all that he needs and wants, the question of distributive justice no longer arises.[14] This, then, is the context in which we must reappraise the economists' focus on production.

Nineteenth-century economic theory, facing a situation of widespread insufficiency, tended to dwell morbidly on the agonizing difficulties of distribution. Economic textbooks concerned themselves at discouraging length with the issues that arise in determining the proper allotment of the economic product among the four major claimant groups: capitalist, manager, worker, and landowner. Economists of the twentieth century, confronted by technological and managerial advances of an unprecedented kind, see before them (in advanced countries, at any rate) not only the potential for, but increasingly the actuality of abundance. To press for the increasing realization of this prospect is to advance the cause of production to the point where problems of distribution become less pressing and increasingly even less relevant. Thus, under the circumstances before them, there is substantial justification, even from the standpoint of distributive justice, for the modern welfare economists' priority of production over distribution. Despite room for grave misgivings about their avowed reasons for choosing it, one cannot but admit that there is substantial justification for the course they have chosen to pursue. From this point of view, we see our present discussion

---

[14] David Hume put the matter thus: "If nature supplied abundantly all our wants and desires . . . the jealousy of interest, which justice supposes, could no longer have a place." *Treatise of Human Nature,* Book III, sec. 2.

as setting forth the philosophical rationale for that de-ethiciza-
tion of economics which no one desires more eagerly than the
economists themselves.

10. A Further Look at Distributive Justice in an Economy of Abundance: Windfalls

Some key issues in the theory of distributive justice, especially
questions of distribution in an economy of abundance, can be
examined with greater precision if more detailed heed is paid
to the way in which the relative claims of those involved are
determined. In particular, it is important to distinguish between (1) *sliding-scale claims* whose magnitude is variable in
terms of the total available for distribution, and (2) *fixed
amount claims* whose magnitude is constant. An instance of
the former is provided when A's share is specified as being
twice B's (i.e., A's claims are twice as large as B's). An instance
of fixed-amount claims is provided when A's claims are determined to amount to a fixed quantity X, and B's a fixed quantity Y, these amounts being determined without regard to the
actual total that is available for distribution. Somewhat generally and loosely, relative claims based on need tend to be
fixed-amount claims (each needs a certain amount and then
their need becomes satisfied at that point) while relative
claims based on desert tend to be sliding-scale claims (one's
merit gives him half or twice the claim of another—without
any reference to amounts).

From the angle of distributive justice, the assessment of
distributions in the case of sliding-scale claims poses little difficulty: given the total amount, we use the sliding scale to determine the ideal distribution, and select our preferred distribution in terms of closeness to this ideal. But the case of

fixed-amount claims is a more difficult one, for there will obviously be three very different possible situations, according as
the amount actually available for distribution is (i) *equal to*
the sum total of the claims of the parties to the distribution
(making for an economy of sufficiency), (ii) *less than* the sum
total of the claims (making for an economy of scarcity), (iii)
more than the sum total of the claims (making for an economy of abundance). In case (i), there is once again no difficulty: the principle of proportionality serves unproblemati-
cally as a guide to the assessment of distributions. In case (ii),
difficulties arise for the theory of distributive justice only at
the point at which the proportionality rule must give way to
the workings of a principle of catastrophe-prevention. The
issues at stake here have already been dealt with at some
length. Case (iii), however, poses a new difficulty of substantial
interest: the problem of the disposition of an *unmerited surplus*, a "windfall."

Suppose, for example, that a distribution is to be made
under the following circumstances: three individual claimants
(A, B, and *C)* are involved; their claims are fixed-amount
claims of 15, 20, and 25 units, respectively; the total actually
available for distribution is 120 units. Here then we can (*ex
hypothesi*) satisfy all the claims involved, but have left the
problem of disposing of an unmerited surplus of 60 units.
From the angle of distributive justice, four major alternatives
stand before us:

1) Distribution in accordance with a *straightforward application of the proportionality principle* of shares proportionate
to claims. With the claims standing in the ratio 15:20:25, the
resultant shares would, on this principle, be divided in the
same proportion, and would thus be 30, 40, and 50, respectively.

2) Distribution in line with a *devious application of the
proportionality principle*. We would divide the stock available
for distribution into two parts: (i) the basic "sufficiency" of 60
units needed to cover the existing claims, and (ii) the addi-

tional surplus that is available. The first, basic part would be divided in the obviously proper way in line with the rule of proportionality, and the second, surplus part would be divided equally, with the same principle in mind, since the claims upon it are *ex hypothesi* equal (i.e., all = 0).[15] This rationale of allotment would lead to the distribution 35, 40, and 45.

3) Distribution in line with the idea of *an escalation of minima*. We would reason thus: "Consider as a starting point the distribution of (1) above. Surely here the rich (viz., *C*) gets too much and the poor (viz., *A*) too little of the 'windfall.' " Under the circumstances what we must do is introduce a pseudo-minimum (say, of 33 units under these circumstances [16]) and make those who are "well off" pay the price (presumably in a pro rata way) of meeting these minima.[17] This rationale of allotment would lead to the distribution 33, 39, and 48.

4) Distribution in accordance with the *rule of strict equality*, whenever this does not lead to anyone's getting less than the amount of his claim. (Actually, this principle could be assimilated to the preceding one in line with the conception that in such windfall cases, a "pseudo-minimum" should be set at $1/n$th of the total when there are n participants in the division.) In the case at hand this would of course result in three equal shares of 40 units each.

It is clear that markedly different ideologies of distribution manifest themselves in these alternative approaches to the question of dividing a windfall. A more claims-minded ap-

---

[15] Exactly this was the rationale of gas rationing in the United Kingdom in World War II. The allotment consisted of a primary allocation based on need and a surplus allotment giving equal mileage to all car owners.

[16] That is, something like 10 per cent over and above the minimal share according to the distribution of type (1) above.

[17] In a way, this procedure amounts to an abandonment of the "fixed-amount" status of the initial claims, and amounts, in effect, to a readjustment of the schedule of claims in the light of the total available for distribution.

proach to justice would tend to favor principles (1) and (2), while a more egalitarian approach would tend to favor (3) and (4).

Any one of these four procedures is more or less plausible. Their diversity confronts us with a certain indeterminacy in our assessment of the distributive justice of the situation, but such indeterminacy should not surprise us when the discussion is pursued at the level of generality to which we must here perforce adhere. The relative merits of these principles cannot be assessed *in abstracto,* but require detailed reference to the particular sorts of claims at issue.

Actually, a somewhat surprising thing is that these very general considerations of distributive justice lead to as definite a result as they in fact do. For what we can say is that since the schedule of claims

$A:$ 15 units
$B:$ 20 units
$C:$ 25 units

leads, from the several appropriate points of view, to the following range of alternatives:

	SCHEME i	SCHEME ii	SCHEME iii	SCHEME iv
$A:$	30 units	35 units	33 units	40 units
$B:$	40	40	39	40
$C:$	50	45	48	40

an acceptable distribution in the case at hand must conform to the following general pattern:

$A:$ 30-40 units
$B:$ 39-40 units
$C:$ 40-50 units

In the light of this, we are entitled to say something quite specific about the three following distribution schemes, supposing these to be the only ones to be feasible or practical under the circumstances:

	SCHEME I	SCHEME II	SCHEME III
A:	29 units	20 units	55 units
B:	40	45	35
C:	51	55	30

Under the specified conditions, from the standpoint of distributive justice, Scheme I is clearly preferable to either of the others, while Scheme II is clearly preferable to III. And, incidentally, the given analysis shows how in some cases practical agreement is possible in the face of a wide variety of ideological differences: when the only practically available alternatives are Schemes I, II, and III, all four approaches to the problem of windfall division will agree upon the preferability of Scheme I (although, it should be noted, all of the schemes satisfy the basic schedule of claims).

6

The Proper Sphere of the Principle of Utility

1. *Reconsideration of the Principle*

The time is now at hand for a return to the principle of utility exhorting "the greatest good of the greatest number." Our opening chapters cast a critical eye upon the utilitarian principle of distribution taken as the criterion of distributive justice, and found it wanting in various respects. These respects for the most part revolved about the question of individual claims, an issue we found it necessary to pursue at some length. The utilitarian principle must now be reconsidered in the light of our subsequent analysis of the role of claims. An inquiry should, in simple fairness, be made with regard to what can be said for the principle of utility as a standard of distributive justice.

2. *The Criticisms of the Principle Rehearsed*

Our critique of the utilitarian formula, apart from dwelling upon the need for removing certain ambiguities in the principle itself, turned primarily upon two points: (1) The need to qualify the principle by an added principle of catastrophe-avoidance to minimize the number of persons who are to be recipients of a subminimal share. (2) The need to restrict the direct applicability of the principle to the case of equal claims (or else to supplement it by other principles to yield a resultant set of principles adequate to cases of differential claims). Any utilitarian theory of distributive justice that is not prepared to accept such qualifications seems to do violence to our sense of justice.

The defense of a qualified utilitarianism has been common in the recent literature of philosophical ethics. But it is essential to realize just how extensive and drastic the needed qualifications will have to be if the resulting version of the utilitarian principle is to be secured against the sorts of strictures we have adduced.

One significant attempt has been to amend the principle of utility in this way, that when *other things are equal,* one should indeed choose that alternative distribution which affords "the greatest good of the greatest number." It would be maintained that when other things (including primarily and specifically considerations of claims, equity, and justice) bear equally upon the alternatives, the one that best meets the requirements of the principle of utility is to be preferred.[1] In this weakened form of (let us call it) *"ceteris paribus* utilitarianism," the utilitarian position seems to be innocuous enough. (It should be noted that for the position as amended the distinction between act- and rule-utilitarianism becomes otiose.) It must however be recognized that this weakened position has wholly given up maintaining what is surely the key tenet of classical utilitarianism, to wit, the contention that considerations of justice and fairness are of *subordinate* status to considerations of utility because they can be *derived* from the principle of utility. The qualified utilitarianism at issue recognizes them as *needed supplements drawn from an en-*

[1] This position is supported by W. K. Frankena in his *Ethics* (Englewood Cliffs, N. J.: Prentice-Hall, 1963), p. 35.

tirely different set of considerations, and not as merely subordinate derivatives at all.

And even this attenuated version of utilitarianism needs further qualification. For consider again the previous example (Chapter Three, pp. 53–54) of two alternative divisions of utility shares among thoroughly but equally wicked individuals of exactly identical status with respect to claims:

SCHEME I	SCHEME II
Equal but small shares	Equal but larger shares

Here is a case of a choice between the alternatives where all "other things" are (*ex hypothesi*) fully equal, but yet the principle of utility's insistence upon adoption of Scheme II is unpalatable, or at any rate disputable. A valid application of the utilitarian principle must be based upon an explicit deservingness postulate.

These qualifications leave the principle of utility in a curtailed—one might almost say *mutilated*—state. For as regards distributive justice, utility is now no longer the touchstone, the final criterion, the ultimate arbiter. It must move over to make room for an associate that is fully independent and coequal with it, to wit, justice. Justice is not to be subordinated to utility; utility must be coordinated with justice. The principle of utility thus meets the fate of inadequacy awaiting so many of the simplicistic one-track *summum bonum* theories of philosophical ethics.

3. *The Applicability of the Principle of Utility Reappraised*

On our analysis of the matter there are circumstances, very special but nevertheless important circumstances, under which the principle of utility can validly be applied. These special circumstances will be exactly those under which the two previously developed lines of criticism will prove inapplicable. For suppose (1) that we have to do with a "utility economy" that is not one of scarcity, and (2) that we have an essentially fixed amount of "utility" to distribute (so that there is no way of benefiting all by adopting a less equitable alternative division of a larger amount) among a group of potential recipients whose claims are essentially identical, and all of whom are "deserving." In this circumstance the principle of utility, construed to embody something like the least-square equity principle of Chapter Two, qualifies as a plausible principle of choice among alternative distributions.

Now the qualifications of circumstances (1) and (2) are not so restrictive as it might seem. They are realized in a very important context, namely, that of *the state* under the circumstances prevailing in modern times in Europe and North America. Given an essentially fixed budget of goods and evils to dispose of, given that the goods at issue are being distributed in response to unearned claims rather than earned ones (as with, say, military decorations), given that scarcity conditions do not prevail, given a political theory of equality that views the state as, in general, free from the involvement of special responsibilities toward some (unlike, say, a parent) so that all are "equal under the law," and given that the state cannot but treat all its people as in principle "deserving," [2] all the requisite conditions are met. The sphere of the principle of utility is, as Bentham wished it, that of legislation. The prize target of the maxim "the greatest good of the greatest number" is the *legislator* (in his official role)—not the employer, the teacher, or the paterfamilias.

[2] Surely one of the most fundamental consequences of the secularization of the state in modern times in the West is that, law-abidingness and personal sacrifice for the public good apart, the state is simply not entitled to moral judgments about its citizens. Contrast the position of Moses *vis à vis* the Children of Israel at Sinai.

From the standpoint of distributive justice, then, the principle of utility is most unsatisfactory as a principle of personal morality guiding day-to-day choices in individual conduct, but eminently suitable as a legislative maxim—a regulative principle for the legislative branch of government—under the conditions that prevail in an economically advanced modern society with respect to certain distributions in the context of unmerited claims. Let me explain. The distributions of certain goods (and evils) can, to an extent, be viewed as the disposal of a "social product." This social product is the fruit of institutions (e.g., schools) and facilities (e.g., financial instrumentalities) embodying the labor of past generations in such a way that they represent currently available assets whose advantages are, in significant measure, "unmerited" by members of the present generation. In such an intricately articulated economy, various "public assets" (and public liabilities also) can be regarded as available to the state—rather than to certain individuals—for distribution or redistribution (e.g., on the negative side through taxation or military service, and on the positive side by creating such "public facilities" as national parks or such "public works" as urban renewal).[8] Within this special range, the principle of utility may plausibly be given undisputed sway. This is particularly obvious in cases in which claims do not enter and where desert is obviously irrelevant (because the deserving and the undeserving—

8 To say this is not to deny that the state may, under modern economic and social circumstances in the West, be a highly inefficient agent of redistribution. In the United States, the highly graduated income tax has not been notably successful, to put it mildly. Cf. R. A. Dahl and C. E. Lindblom, *Politics, Economics, and Welfare* (New York: Harper & Bros., 1953), pp. 135–136. Moreover, this line of support of state-redistribution is one whose validity obtains only within circumscribed limits that are easily overstepped. We concur in the view of B. de Jouvenel: "The method of so-called redistribution through the agency of the redistributing State, and its outcome, the favouring of corporate bodies over individuals, seems to us to pertain to a vast evolutionary process which will not result in equality, and in which the egalitarian ideal is put to work, in all good faith, for ends other than itself" (*The Ethics of Redistribution*, p. 81).

whoever they be—are all "in the same boat"). One should think here of the great mass of social measures which must in the very nature of things under modern conditions of life pretty well benefit everyone alike: fire protection, air-pollution control, traffic safety, mail service, public health, etc.

4. Justice as Limit upon Utility

The impetus of our argument has been expended in two directions. Against doctrinaire utilitarianism we have argued the inadequacy of a theory of distribution that ignores justice by failing to take claims into due and appropriate account. Against doctrinaire insistence upon justice construed strictly in terms of fairness we have urged the unacceptability of the *fiat justitia ruat caelum* line of thinking. The pivotal concept of our position is *coordination*, that an acceptable theory of distribution requires the due meshing of considerations of justice (in the narrow sense of fairness and equity) with those of utility (in the sense of the general welfare). Regarding the rationale of distributive justice, our position is neither strictly deontological nor strictly utilitarian: it is a *deontological utilitarianism*. If this is objected to as "a somewhat unsatisfactory dualism," [4] the reply must be that such a complex position is inescapable in a case in which a "satisfactory monism" is, in the nature of things, impossible.

An important limitation of our approach has been stressed from the outset: it is retrospective and externalized. We have not considered distributions as changes made within the setting of an ongoing historical process. Nevertheless, our considerations to some extent have a bearing on this case also, particularly regarding the importance for justice of a recognition of claims. In a concrete historical context, after all, one of the

[4] As the author of the article on Henry Sidgwick in the 11th edition of the *Encyclopedia Britannica* objects against Sidgwick on another subject.

distributions within the range of alternatives is the actual, *existing* distribution, and this distribution is a very important one, from the standpoint of distributive justice. Only God can shape a world *de novo;* we mortals have to *start from where we are* within "a world we did not make." Other distributions may well be (no, unquestionably are) superior to the existing one, but "we can only get there from here" by reshaping an existing situation. And this existing situation carries within it an existing body of claims, claims which must, in the interests of justice, be taken into account. Justice limits utility at exactly the point of the "Reformer's Paradox": Given an imperfect existing initial distribution, any redistribution in the interests of arriving, from the standpoint of justice, at a superior distribution runs headlong into the pattern of existing claims that cannot—in the interests of the very justice that provides the rationale for the entire enterprise—be brushed aside as an irrelevant obstacle.

5. Conclusion

We have now come to the end of our journey. In the course of the inquiry it has become apparent that the most that can be done for the "principle of utility" is to regard it as characterizing what is from the standpoint of ethical theory no more than a point of prima facie merit. To be that alternative which represents a distribution of goods according to the rule of "greater good of a greater number" is to exhibit a trait that can *provisionally* be regarded as a point of merit, in the absence of further and very possibly countervailing considerations. But in taking this view of the Principle of Utility in the context of the problem of distributive justice, the principle is forced to abdicate its throne as the basic arbiter, the sole, ultimate criterion. Utility is no longer the queen bee, but becomes merely one among several workers in the ethical hive.

Bibliography

To use this Bibliography one should understand what it does and does not set out to do. It has three main limitations. (1) From the aspect of the social sciences, except for the topic of distributive justice proper, the aim is to be representative rather than complete. (2) Regarding the historical (pre-twentieth-century) sector of the philosophical aspect, the aim is to be informative rather than definitive, except that (3) the evolutionary ethics of Darwin, Spencer, and their numerous successors is taken to fall outside the purview of treatment. Consequently there is an attempt at comprehensive coverage only in twentieth-century *philosophical* discussions of utilitarianism, and in extensive twentieth-century treatments of the ethical problems of distributive justice.

A. General Historical Surveys

Albee, Ernest. *A History of English Utilitarianism.* New York: Macmillan, 1902.

Bonar, James. *Philosophy and Political Economy.* London: Swann Sonnenschild, 1893.

Davidson, William Leslie. *Political Thought in England: the Utilitarians from Bentham to J. S. Mill.* Oxford: Oxford University Press, 1915.

Gide, C., and C. Rist. *A History of Economic Doctrines from the Time of the Physiocrats to the Present Day.* Tr. R. Richards. Boston: Heath & Co., 1938. 2nd edn., 1948.

Graham, William. *English Politics from Hobbes to Maine.* London: E. Arnold, 1899.

Guyau, M. *La morale anglaise contemporaine: morale de l'utilité et de l'évolution.* Paris: F. Alcan, 1879.

Halévy, Elie. *The Growth of Philosophic Radicalism.* Tr. Mary Morris. London: Faber & Gwyer, 1928.

Hicks, G. Dawes. "Die englische Philosophie." In T. K. Oesterreich, ed., *Friederich Ueberwegs Grundriss der Geschichte der Philosophie.* Part 5, *Die Philosophie des Auslandes vom Beginn des 19. Jahrhunderts.* 12th edn. Berlin: E. S. Mittler u. Sohn, 1928.

Höffding, Harald. *A History of Modern Philosophy.* 2 vols. London: Macmillan, 1900.

Kaler, Emil. *Die Ethik des Utilitarianisms.* Hamburg and Leipzig: L. Voss, 1885. Inaugural dissertation for Basel University.

MacCunn, John. *Six Radical Thinkers.* London: E. Arnold, 1910.

Metz, Rudolf. *A Hundred Years of Philosophy.* New York: Macmillan, 1938. See ch. 2, pp. 47–93.

Mondolfo, R. *Saggi per la storia della morale utilitaria.* 2 vols. Verona and Padova: Drucker, 1903–1904.

Passmore, John. *One Hundred Years of Philosophy.* London: Macmillan, 1957.

Plamenatz, J. *The English Utilitarians.* Oxford: The Clarendon Press, 1958.

Price, L. L. *Political Economy in England from Adam Smith to Arnold Toynbee.* London: Methuen and Co., 1890.

Robertson, J. M. *A Short History of Morals.* London: Watts & Co., 1920.

Rossi, M. M. "Utilitarismo," *Enciclopedia Filosofica,* Vol. IV. Venezia: Instituto per la collaborazione culturale, 1957–1958.

Sabine, George. *A History of Political Theory*. New York: Holt, Rinehart and Winston, 1961. See pp. 669–755.

Selby-Bigge, L. A. *British Moralists*. Oxford: The Clarendon Press, 1897.

Somervell, David C. *English Thought in the Nineteenth Century*. New York: Longmans Green, 1936.

Sorley, W. R. *A History of English Philosophy*. Cambridge: Cambridge University Press, 1920.

Stephen, Sir Leslie. *The English Utilitarians*. 3 vols. London: Duckworth & Co., 1900. Reprinted in 1 vol., New York: Peter Smith, 1950.

B. *Precursors of Utilitarianism*

Among the more prominent precursors of utilitarianism since the eighteenth century are the following. Details regarding the relevant contributions of these men can be found in every good encyclopedia and history of philosophy.

(1) JOHN GAY (1669–1745)
(2) BERNARD DE MANDEVILLE (1670–1733)
(3) FRANCIS HUTCHESON (1694–1747)
(4) DAVID HARTLEY (1705–1757)
(5) ABRAHAM TUCKER (1705–1774)
(6) DAVID HUME (1711–1776)
(7) JOHN BROWN (1715–1766)
(8) CLAUDE ADRIEN HELVETIUS (1715–1771)
(9) ETIENNE CONDILLAC (1715–1780)
(10) EDMUND BURKE (1729?–1797)
(11) JOSEPH PRIESTLEY (1733–1804)
(12) THOMAS PAINE (1737–1809)
(13) CASARE BECCARIA BONESANA (1738–1794)
(14) WILLIAM GODWIN (1756–1836)
(15) THOMAS ROBERT MALTHUS (1766–1834)

C. Classical Utilitarian Theorists and Interpreters

1) WILLIAM PALEY (1743–1805)

Paley, William. *The Principles of Moral and Political Philosophy.* London: 1786; new edn., London: Longman, Orne & Co., 1841.

Bain, A. *The Moral Philosophy of Paley.* London: W. & R. Chambers, 1852.

Whately, Richard. *Paley's Moral Philosophy: With Annotations.* London: John W. Parker & Sons, 1859.

See also any of the works of Section A.

2) JEREMY BENTHAM (1748–1832)

For Bentham's own writings and the earlier literature about him, see the Bibliography in:

Hicks, G. Dawes. "Die englische Philosophie." In T. K. Oesterreich, ed., *Friederich Ueberwegs Grundriss der Geschichte der Philosophie.* Part 5, *Die Philosophie des Auslandes vom Beginn des 19. Jahrhunderts.* 12th edn., Berlin: E. S. Mittler u. Sohn, 1928. Pp. 92, 184.

A more comprehensive bibliography of Bentham (prepared by C. W. Everett) can be found in:

Halévy, Elie. *The Growth of Philosophic Radicalism.* Tr. Mary Morris. London: Faber & Gwyer, 1928.

Some more recent contributions are:

Baumgardt, David. *Bentham and the Ethics of Today.* Princeton: Princeton University Press, 1952.

Burne, P. "Bentham and the Utilitarian Principle," *Mind*,
LVIII (1949), 367–368.

Keeton, George Williams, ed. *Jeremy Bentham and the Law:
A Symposium*. London: Stevens & Sons, 1948.

Mack, Mary Peter. *Jeremy Bentham: An Odyssey of Ideas*.
New York: Columbia University Press, 1963.

Ogden, C. K. Introduction to his edition of Bentham's *The
Theory of Legislation*. London: Routledge & Kegan Paul,
1931. French edn., Trubner & Co., 1931.

Palmer, P. A. "Benthamism in England and America," *American Political Science Review*, XXXV (1941), 855 ff.

Viner, Jacob. *The Long View and the Short View*. "Bentham
and J. S. Mill: The Utilitarian Background." Glencoe,
Ill.: The Free Press, 1953.

See also the works of Section A.

3) JAMES MILL (1773–1836)

For Mill's own writings and the earlier literature about
him, see the Bibliography in G. Dawes Hicks, *op. cit.*,
pp. 91, 184.

See also the works of Section A.

4) JOHN AUSTIN (1790–1859)

For Austin's own writings, see the Bibliography in G.
Dawes Hicks, *op. cit.*, p. 94.

5) JOHN STUART MILL (1806–1873)

For Mill's own writings and the earlier literature about
him, see the Bibliography in G. Dawes Hicks, *op. cit.*,
pp. 94, 184–185. Two valuable bibliographies of more
recent vintage are:

Cranston, Maurice. *John Stuart Mill.* Writers and Their Works Series, no. 99. New York: British Book Center, 1960.

Schneewind, J. B., ed. *Mill's Critical Writings.* New York: Collier Books, 1965.

For an essentially complete Bibliography of Mill's own writings, see:

MacMuin, N., J. R. Hainds, and J. McNab. *Bibliography of the Published Writings of John Stuart Mill.* Northwestern University Studies in the Humanities, no. 12. Evanston: Northwestern University Press, 1945.

Some more recent contributions are:

Aiken, Henry David. *Reason and Conduct.* Ch. 14, "Utilitarianism and Liberty: John Stuart Mill's Defense of Freedom." New York: Alfred A. Knopf, 1962.

Anschutz, R. P. *Philosophy of J. S. Mill.* New York: Oxford University Press, 1953.

Britton, Karl. *John Stuart Mill.* Baltimore: Pelican Books, 1959.

Casellato, S. *Giovanni S. Mill e l'Utilitarismo Inglese.* Padova: Cedam, 1951.

Douglas, C. *Ethics of John Stuart Mill.* Edinburgh: W. Blackwood and Sons, 1897.

Downie, R. S. "Mill on Pleasure and Self-Development," *Philosophical Quarterly,* XVI (1966), 69–71.

Ferri, F. *L'utilitarismo di [John] Stuart Mill.* Milano, 1892.

Lindsay, A. D. Introduction to *Mill's Utilitarianism, Liberty and Representative Government.* New York: Dutton, 1950.

Mabbott, J. D. "Interpretations of Mill's 'Utilitarianism,'" *Philosophical Quarterly,* VI (1956), 115.

McCloskey, H. J. "Mill's Liberalism," *Philosophical Quarterly,* XIII (1963), 143–156.

Plamenatz, John. *Mill's Utilitarianism.* New York: Macmillan, 1949.

Rees, John Collwyn. *Mill and His Early Critics*. Leicester: University College Press, 1956.

Russell, Bertrand. "John Stuart Mill," *Proceedings of the British Academy*, IV (1955), 43–59.

Urmson, J. O. "The Interpretation of the Moral Philosophy of J. S. Mill," *Philosophical Quarterly*, III (1953), 33–39.

See also works of Section A. On "Mill's Fallacy," see Section F4 below.

6) HENRY SIDGWICK (1838–1900)

For Sidgwick's own writings and earlier literature about him, see G. Dawes Hicks, *op. cit.*, pp. 102, 186.

Some more recent contributions are:

Broad, C. D. "Henry Sidgwick." In *Ethics and the History of Philosophy*. London: Routledge & Kegan Paul, 1952.

——. *Five Types of Ethical Theory*. Ch. 6, "Sidgwick." London: Routledge & Kegan Paul, 1930.

Lacey, J. R. "Sidgwick's Ethical Maxims," *Philosophy*, XXXIX (1959), 217–228.

Sinclair, A. G. *Der Utilitarismus bei Sidgwick und Spencer*. Heidelberg: C. Winter, 1907.

See also works of Section A.

D. Major Critics of Utilitarianism

1) NINETEENTH-CENTURY INTUITIONISTS AND IDEALISTS

Bradley, F. H. *Ethical Studies*. London: M. S. King & Son, 1876. 2nd edn., Oxford: The Clarendon Press, 1927. See especially Essay III, "Pleasure for Pleasure's Sake."

——. *Mr. Sidgwick's Hedonism*. London: M. S. King & Son, 1877.

Douglas, Charles. *The Ethics of John Stuart Mill*. London: W. Blackwood and Sons, 1897.

Green, T. H. *Prolegomena to Ethics*. Oxford: The Clarendon Press, 1890. See especially Book IV.

———. *Lectures on the Principles of Political Obligation*. London: Longmans Green, 1941.

Grote, John. *An Examination of the Utilitarian Philosophy*. Cambridge: Deighton, Bell, 1870.

———. *A Treatise on the Moral Ideals*. Cambridge: Cambridge University Press, 1876.

Hartmann, Nicolai. *Ethics*. Vol. I, ch. 9 (pp. 131–159). "Eudaemonism and Utilitarianism." Tr. Stanton Coit. London: George Allen & Unwin, 1958. Initially published as *Das Sittliche Bewusstsein*, Leipzig, 1926.

Jevons, W. S. *Pure Logic and Other Minor Works*. London: Macmillan, 1890. (Miscellaneous essays touch on Mill's ethics.)

McCosh, James. *An Examination of J. S. Mill's Philosophy*. London: Macmillan, 1866.

———. *The Present State of Moral Philosophy in England*. London: Macmillan, 1868.

Makintosh, James. *A General View of the Progress of Ethical Philosophy*. Philadelphia: Carey & Lea, 1832.

Martineau, James. *Types of Ethical Theory*. Vol. II, ch. 2, "Utilitarian Hedonism." 3rd edn., revised. Oxford: The Clarendon Press, 1901.

Rashdall, Hastings. "Prof. Sidgwick's Utilitarianism," *Mind*, O.S., X (1885), 200–226.

———. "Can There be a Sum of Pleasures?" *Mind*, VIII (1899), 357–382.

———. *Theory of Good and Evil*. Oxford: The Clarendon Press, 1907. 2nd edn., 1924.

Spencer, Herbert. *The Data of Ethics*. London: Williams & Norgate, 1879. See especially ch. 13.

Stephen, James Fitzjames. *Liberty, Equality, Fraternity*. London: Smith, Elder & Co., 1873.

Watson, J. *Hedonistic Theories*. Glasgow: J. Maclehose & Sons, 1895.

2) TWENTIETH-CENTURY PRAGMATISTS AND ANALYSTS

Dewey, John. *Outlines of a Critical Theory of Ethics.* New York: Hillary House, 1957. Secs. 19–25 (pp. 42–72).

——, and James Tufts. *Ethics.* New York: Henry Holt, 1908. See pp. 263–306.

Lewis, C. I. *An Analysis of Knowledge and Valuation.* Ch. 16, sec. 4, "Critique of Benthamite Calculus of Values." La Salle: Open Court, 1950. See all of chs. 16–17.

Mitchell, W. C. "Bentham's Felicific Calculus," *Political Science Quarterly,* XXXIII (1918), 161–183.

Moore, G. E. *Ethics.* London: Oxford University Press, 1911. Reset 1947. See especially chs. 1 and 2.

——. *Principia Ethica.* Cambridge: Cambridge University Press, 1903.

Prichard, H. A. "Does Moral Philosophy Rest on a Mistake?" and "Moral Obligation." In *Moral Obligation.* Oxford: The Clarendon Press, 1957. (Criticism from an intuitionist perspective.)

Ross, W. D. *The Right and the Good.* Oxford: The Clarendon Press, 1930.

——. *Foundations of Ethics.* London: Oxford University Press, 1939.

Schlick, Moritz. *Problems of Ethics.* Ch. 4, secs. 3–6. New York: Dover Publications, 1962.

E. Later Commentaries and Expositions

1) TO 1900

Birks, T. R. *Modern Utilitarianism.* London: Macmillan, 1874.

Gizycki, Georg von. *Die Ethik David Hume's.* Appendix, "Über die universelle Glückseligkeit als oberstes Moralprincip." Breslau: Louis Koehler, 1878.

Edgeworth, F. Y. *Mathematical Psychics.* London: Kegan Paul, 1881. Reprinted, New York: A. M. Kelly, 1961.

2) AFTER 1900

Laird, John. *An Enquiry into Moral Notions.* London: George Allen & Unwin, 1935. See ch. 17.

Stace, Walter Terence. *The Concept of Morals.* New York: Macmillan, 1937. See chs. 7 and 10.

Garin, E. *L'illuminismo inglese: i moralisti.* Milano: Fratelli Bocca, 1941.

Swabey, W. C. "Non-Normative Utilitarianism," *Journal of Philosophy,* XL (1943), 365–374.

Ayer, A. J. "The Principle of Utility." In *Jeremy Bentham and the Law.* G. W. Keeton and G. Schwarzenberger, eds. London: Stevens & Sons, 1948. Reprinted in A. J. Ayer, *Philosophical Essays.* London: Macmillan, 1954.

Ewing, A. C. "Utilitarianism," *Ethics,* LVIII (1948), 100–111.

McGreal, Ian. "A Naturalistic Utilitarianism," *Journal of Philosophy,* XLVII (1950), 520–526.

Melden, A. I. "Two Comments on Utilitarianism," *Philosophical Review,* LX (1951), 519–523.

Broad, C. D. *Ethics and the History of Philosophy.* London: Routledge & Kegan Paul, 1952.

Brown, S. M., Jr., "Duty and the Production of Good," *Philosophical Review,* LXI (1952), 299–330.

Garnett, Arthur Campbell. *The Moral Nature of Man: A Critical Evaluation of Ethical Principles.* New York: Ronald Press, 1952.

Schneider, H. W. "Utilitarianism and Moral Obligation," *Philosophical Review,* LXI (1952), 299–319. (This is the leading paper of a symposium with comments by John Ladd, pp. 320–326, and C. A. Baylis, pp. 327–330.)

Wedar, Sven. *Duty and Utility: A Study in English Moral Philosophy.* Lund, Sweden: C. W. K. Gleerup, 1952.

Ewing, A. C. *Ethics*. London: English Universities Press, 1953.

Garvin, Lucius. *A Modern Introduction to Ethics*. New York: Houghton Mifflin, 1953. See chs. 10–11 on utilitarianism, and ch. 16 on social justice.

Clark, Pamela. "Some Difficulties in Utilitarianism," *Philosophy*, XXIX (1954), 244–252.

Nowell-Smith, P. H. *Ethics*. London: Penguin Books, 1954. See pp. 232–239, 271–273.

Hourani, George F. *Ethical Value*. Ann Arbor: University of Michigan Press, 1956. See pp. 35–37, 125–126, 136–139, 145–152.

Rein'l, Robert. "The Limits of Utility," *Journal of Philosophy*, LIII (1956), 549–556.

MacKinnon, D. M. *A Study in Ethical Theory*. Ch. 2, "Utilitarianism" (pp. 22–60). London: Adam & Charles Black, 1957.

Penelhum, T. "The Logic of Pleasure," *Philosophy and Phenomenological Research*, XVII (1956–1957), 488–503.

Baier, Kurt. *The Moral Point of View*. Ithaca: Cornell University Press, 1958.

Smart, R. N. "Negative Utilitarianism," *Mind*, LXVII (1958), 542–543.

Brandt, R. B. *Ethical Theory*. Englewood Cliffs: Prentice-Hall, 1959. See ch. 15.

Ewing, A. C. *Second Thoughts in Moral Philosophy*. London: Routledge & Kegan Paul, 1959. See especially pp. 104 ff. and pp. 130 ff.

Johnson, Oliver. *Rightness and Goodness*. The Hague: M. Nijhoff, 1959.

Britton, Karl. "Utilitarianism: The Appeal to a First Principle," *Aristotelian Society Proceedings*, LX (1959–1960), 141–154.

Toulmin, S. E. *The Place of Reason in Ethics*. London: Cambridge University Press, 1960.

Findlay, J. N. *Values and Intentions*. Ch. 6, "Values of Welfare," and ch. 7, "Injustice and its Disvalues." London: George Allen & Unwin, 1961.

Hospers, John. *Human Conduct*. New York: Harcourt, Brace & World, 1961. See pp. 199–240 and 311–343.

Singer, Marcus George. *Generalization in Ethics*. Ch. 7, "Moral Principles and the Principle of Utility" (pp. 178–216). New York: Alfred A. Knopf, 1961.

Smart, J. J. C. *An Outline of a System of Utilitarian Ethics*. Victoria: Melbourne University Press, 1961.

Anderson, John. *Studies in Empirical Philosophy*. Ch. 20, "Utilitarianism" (pp. 227–237). Sydney: Angus and Robertson, 1962.

Popper, K. *Conjectures and Refutations*. New York: Basic Books, 1962.

Acton, H. B., and J. W. N. Watkins. Symposium: "Negative Utilitarianism," *Aristotelian Society Proceedings*, Supp. Vol. XXXVII (1963), 83–114.

Brandt, Richard B. "Toward a Credible Form of Utilitarianism." In *Morality and the Language of Conduct*. H. Castaneda and G. Nakhnikan, eds. Detroit: Wayne State University Press, 1963.

Braybrooke, David, and Charles E. Lindblom. *A Strategy of Decision*. Part 4, "The Rehabilitation of Utilitarianism." New York: The Free Press of Glencoe, 1963.

D'Arcy, Eric. *Human Acts*. Oxford: The Clarendon Press, 1963. See pp. 57–85, 167–170.

Hare, R. M. *Freedom and Reason*. Ch. 7, "Utilitarianism" (pp. 112–136). Oxford: The Clarendon Press, 1963.

Popper, K. *The Open Society and its Enemies*. 4th edn., revised. Princeton: Princeton University Press, 1963.

Lyons, D. *Forms and Limits of Utilitarianism*. Oxford: The Clarendon Press, 1965.

Narveson, Jan. "Utilitarianism and Formalism," *Australasian Journal of Philosophy*, XLIII (1965), 58–72.

F. Specialized Topics

1) UTILITARIAN THEORY OF JUSTICE

Harrison, J. "Utilitarianism, Universalisation and Our Duty to be Just," *Proceedings of the Aristotelian Society*, LIII (1952–1953) , 105–134.

Raphael, D. Daiches. *Moral Judgment*. Ch. 5, "Justice" (pp. 62–94) . London: George Allen & Unwin, 1955.

Hall, Everett M. "Justice as Fairness: A Modernized Version of the Social Contract," *Journal of Philosophy*, LIV (1957) , 662–670.

Bedau, Hugo. "Justice and Classical Utilitarianism." In *Justice*. Carl Friedrich, ed. New York: Atherton Press, 1963.

Chapman, John. "Justice and Fairness." In *Justice*. Carl Friedrich, ed. New York: Atherton Press, 1963.

Eckhoff, Torstein. "Justice and Social Utility." In *Legal Essays: A Tribute to Fred Castberg*. Oslo, 1963, pp. 74–93.

Friedrich, Carl. *Man and His Government*. Ch. 6, "Justice: The Just Political Act." New York: McGraw-Hill, 1963.

Ginsberg, Morris. "The Concept of Justice," *Philosophy*, XXXVIII (1963), 99–116.

Rawls, John. "Constitutional Liberty and the Concept of Justice." In *Justice*, Carl Friedrich, ed. New York: Atherton Press, 1963.

———. "The Sense of Justice," *Philosophical Review*, LXXII (1963), 281–305.

2) UTILITARIAN THEORY OF PUNISHMENT

Ewing, A. C. "Punishment as a Moral Agency, An Attempt to Reconcile the Retributive and the Utilitarian View," *Mind*, XXXVI (1927) , 292–305.

Carritt, Edgar F. *The Theory of Morals: An Introduction to Ethical Philosophy.* New York: Oxford University Press, 1928. See ch. 12.

Ewing, A. C. *The Morality of Punishment.* London: Routledge & Kegan Paul, 1929. See p. 44.

Ross, W. D. "The Ethics of Punishment," *Philosophy,* IV (1929), 205–211.

Mabbott, J. D. "Punishment," *Mind,* XLVIII (1939), 152-167.

MacLagan, W. G. "Punishment and Retribution," *Philosophy,* XIV (1939), 282–298.

Carritt, Edgar F. *Ethical and Political Thinking.* New York: Oxford University Press, 1947. See ch. 5.

Flew, Antony. "The Justification of Punishment," *Philosophy,* XXIX (1954), 291–307.

Mundle, C. W. K. "Punishment and Desert," *Philosophical Quarterly,* IV (1954), 216–228.

Quinton, A. M. "On Punishment," *Analysis,* XIV (1954–1955), 13–16.

Baier, K. "Is Punishment Retributive?" *Analysis,* XVI (1955), 25–32.

Mabbott, J. D. "Free Will and Punishment." In *Contemporary British Philosophy* (pp. 287–309). H. D. Lewis, ed. 3rd Series. London: Allen & Unwin, 1956.

Moser, S. "Utilitarian Theories of Punishment and Moral Judgments," *Philosophical Studies,* VIII (1957), 15–19.

Benn, S. L. "An Approach to the Problems of Punishment," *Philosophy,* XXXIII (1958), 325–341.

Hart, H. L. A. "Prolegomenon to the Principles of Punishment," *Proceedings of the Aristotelian Society,* LX (1959–1960), 1–26.

Stevenson, Charles L. *Ethics and Language.* New Haven: Yale University Press, 1960. See pp. 301–302, 307 ff.

Michael, Jerome, and Herbert Wechsler. *Criminal Law and Its Administration.* Part 1, sec. 2, "Basic Problems of Criminal Law; Ends and Means" (pp. 4–20). Chicago: Foundation Press, 1940. Reprinted in *Value and Obligation*. Richard Brandt, ed. New York: Harcourt, Brace & World, 1961.

McCloskey, H. J. "A Note on Utilitarian Punishment," *Mind,* LXXII (1963), 599.

———. "A Non-Utilitarian Approach to Punishment," *Inquiry,* VIII (1965), 249–263.

Sprigge, T. L. S. "A Utilitarian Reply to Dr. McCloskey," *Inquiry,* VIII (1965), 264–291.

3) ACT- VERSUS RULE-UTILITARIANISM

Harrod, R. F. "Utilitarianism Revised," *Mind,* XLV (1936), 137–156.

Rawls, John. "Outline of a Decision Procedure for Ethics," *Philosophical Review,* LX (1951), 177–197.

Harrison, J. "Utilitarianism, Universalisation and Our Duty to be Just," *Proceedings of the Aristotelian Society,* LIII (1952–1953), 105–134.

MacKinnon, Donald M., ed. *Christian Faith and Communist Faith.* London: Macmillan, 1953.

Urmson, J. O. "The Interpretation of the Moral Philosophy of J. S. Mill," *Philosophical Quarterly,* III (1953), 33–39.

Stout, A. K. "But Suppose Everyone Did the Same," *Australasian Journal of Philosophy,* XXXII (1954), 1–29.

Rawls, John. "Two Concepts of Rules," *Philosophical Review,* LXIV (1955), 3–32.

Mabbott, J. D. "Interpretations of Mill's Utilitarianism," *Philosophical Quarterly,* VI (1956), 115–120.

Smart, J. J. C. "Extreme and Restricted Utilitarianism," *Philosophical Quarterly,* VI (1956), 344–354.

Bradley, M. C. "Professor Smart's 'Extreme and Restricted Utilitarianism,'" *Philosophical Quarterly,* VII (1957), 264–266.

Duncan-Jones, A. "Utilitarianism and Rules," *Philosophical Quarterly,* VII (1957), 364–367.

McCloskey, H. J. "An Examination of Restricted Utilitarianism," *Philosophical Review*, LXVI (1957), 466–485.

Schwayder, D. S. "Moral Rules and Moral Maxims," *Ethics*, LXVII (1957), 269–285.

Black, Max. "Notes on the Meaning of 'Rule,'" *Theoria*, XXIV (1958), 121–122.

Brandt, Richard B. *Ethical Theory.* Englewood Cliffs, N.J.: Van Nostrand, 1959.

Kaplan, Morton A. "Some Problems of the Extreme Utilitarian Position," *Ethics*, LXX (1959–1960), 228-232.

Diggs, B. J. "A Technical Ought," *Mind*, LXIX (1960), 301–317.

Kaplan, Morton A. "Restricted Utilitarianism." *Ethics*, LXXI (1960–1961), 301–302.

Smart, J. J. C. "Extreme Utilitarianism: A Reply to M. A. Kaplan," *Ethics*, LXXI (1960–1961), 133–134.

Wasserstrom, Richard A. *Judicial Decision toward a Theory of Legal Justification.* Stanford: Stanford University Press, 1961.

Broile, R. David. "Is Rule Utilitarianism too Restricted?" *Southern Journal of Philosophy*, II (1964), 180–187.

Diggs, B. J. "Rules and Utilitarianism," *American Philosophical Quarterly*, I (1964), 32–44.

Gauthier, David P. "Rule-utilitarianism and Randomization," *Analysis,* XXV (1965), 68–69.

Lyons, D. *Forms and Limits of Utilitarianism.* Oxford: The Clarendon Press, 1965.

Stearns, J. B. "Ideal Rule Utilitarianism and the Content of Duty," *Kant-studien*, LVI (1965), 53–70.

4)   "DESIRED VERSUS DESIRABLE" ("MILL'S FALLACY")

Seth, James, "The Alleged Fallacies in Mill's Utilitarianism," *Philosophical Review*, XVII (1908), 469–488.

Carritt, E. F. "Thinking Makes it So," *Proceedings of the Aristotelian Society*, XXX (1929–1930), 277-284.

Hall, E. W. "The 'Proof' of Utility in Bentham and Mill," *Ethics*, LX (1949), 1–18.

Popkin, R. H. "A Note on the 'Proof' of Utility in J. S. Mill," *Ethics*, LXI (1950), 66–68.

Aiken, H. D. "Definitions, Factual Premisses, and Ethical Conclusions," *Philosophical Review*, LXI (1952), 331–348.

Urmson, J. O. "The Interpretation of the Moral Philosophy of J. S. Mill," *Philosophical Quarterly*, III (1953), 33–39.

McNaughton, R. "Metric Concept of Happiness," *Philosophy and Phenomenological Research*, XIV (1953–1954), 171–183.

Raphael, D. D. "Fallacies in and about Mill's Utilitarianism," *Philosophy*, XXX (1955), 344–357.

Atkinson, R. F. "J. S. Mill's 'Proof' of the Principle of Utility," *Philosophy*, XXXII (1957), 158–167.

Kretzmann, Norman. "Desire as Proof of Desirability," *Philosophical Quarterly*, VIII (1958), 246–258.

McNeilly, F. S. "Pre-Moral Appraisals," *Philosophical Quarterly*, VIII (1958), 97–111.

Burns, J. H. "Utilitarianism and Democracy," *Philosophical Quarterly*, IX (1959), 168–171.

Stroll, Avrum. "Mill's Fallacy," *Dialogue*, III (1965), 385–404.

G. *Utilitarianism in Economic, Psychological, Sociological, and Political Theory*

1) ECONOMIC UTILITY THEORY

Senior, Nassau. *Four Introductory Lectures on Political Economy*. London: Longmans Green, 1852.

Walras, Léon. *Éléments d'économie politique pure.* 2 vols. Lausanne: L. Corbez & Cie., 1874–1877.

Edgeworth, F. Y. *Mathematical Psychics.* London: Kegan Paul, 1881. Reprinted New York: A. M. Kelly, 1961.

Jevons, W. Stanley. *The Theory of Political Economy.* London: Macmillan, 1885. 4th edn., 1911. See especially ch. 3, "Theory of Utility."

Marshall, Alfred. *Principles of Economics.* London: Macmillan, 1890. 8th edn., 1920. See especially ch. 6 on "Value and Utility."

Keynes, J. N. *The Scope and Method of Political Economy.* London and New York: Macmillan, 1891.

Barone, Enrico. "The Ministry of Production in the Collectivist State." Rome, 1908. Reprinted in *Collectivist Economic Planning* (pp. 245–290). F. A. Hayek, ed. London: Routledge, 1935.

Pareto, Vilfredo. *Manuel d'économie politique.* Tr. from Italian by Alfred Bonnet. Paris: V. Girad & E. Brière, 1909.

Lange, Oscar. "The Determinateness of the Utility Function," *Review of Economic Studies,* I (1934), 218–225.

Sweezy, Alan R. "The Interpretation of Subjective Value Theory in the Writings of the Austrian Economists," *Review of Economic Studies,* I (1934), 176–185.

Pigou, A. C., and N. Georgescu-Roegen. "Marginal Utility of Money and Elasticities of Demand," *Quarterly Journal of Economics,* L (1936), 532–539.

Robbins, Lionel. "Interpersonal Comparisons of Utility: A Comment," *Economic Journal,* XLVIII (1938), 635–641.

Armstrong, W. E. "Uncertainty and the Utility Function," *Economic Journal,* LVIII (1948), 1–10.

Friedman, Milton J., and L. J. Savage. "The Utility Analysis of Choices Involving Risk," *Journal of Political Economy,* LVI (1948), 279–304.

Marshak, Jacob. "Rational Behavior, Uncertain Prospects, and Measurable Utility," *Econometrica*, XVIII (1950), 111–141.

Stigler, George J. "The Development of Utility Theory," *Journal of Political Economy*, LVIII (1950), 307–327, 373–396.

Robertson, D. H. *Utility and All That*. London: Allen & Unwin, 1952.

Georgescu-Roegen, Nicholas. "Choice, Expectations and Measurability," *Quarterly Journal of Economics*, LXVIII (1954), 503–534.

Thrall, Robert M. "Multidimensional Utility Theory." In *Decision Processes*. R. M. Thrall, *et al*. New York: Wiley, 1954.

Harsanyi, John C. "Cardinal Welfare, Individualistic Ethics, and Interpersonal Comparisons of Utility," *Journal of Political Economy*, LXIII (1955), 309–321.

Lipsey, R. G., and Kelvin Lancaster. "The General Theory of the Second Best," *Review of Economic Studies*, XXIV (1956–1957), 11–32.

Rescher, Nicholas. "Notes on Preference, Utility, and Cost," *Synthèse*, XIX (1967).

2) UTILITARIANISM AND ECONOMIC POLICY: WELFARE ECONOMICS

Thompson, William. *Inquiry into the Principles of the Distribution of Wealth*. London: Longman, 1824. 2nd edn., by W. Pare, London: Orr & Co., 1850.

Marshall, Alfred. *Principles of Economics*. London: Macmillan, 1890. 8th edn., 1920. See especially ch. 6 on "Value and Utility."

Wicksteed, Philip Henry. *An Essay on the Co-ordination of the Laws of Distribution*. London: Macmillan, 1894. Photoreprinted, Series of Reprints of Scarce Tracts in Economic and Political Science, no. 12. London School of Economics and Political Science, 1932.

Pareto, Vilfredo. *Manuel d'économie politique.* Tr. Alfred Bonnet. Paris: V. Girad & E. Brière, 1909.

Wicksteed, Philip Henry. *Common Sense of Political Economy.* 1st edn., London: Macmillan, 1910. Revised edn., London: Routledge & Kegan Paul, 1933.

Pigou, A. C. *Wealth and Welfare.* London: Macmillan, 1912.
———. *The Economics of Welfare.* London: Macmillan, 1920. 4th edn., 1932.

Seligman, E. *The Income Tax.* 2nd edn., revised. New York: Macmillan, 1921.
———. *The Shifting and Incidence of Taxation.* 4th edn., revised. New York: Columbia University Press, 1921.

Henderson, H. D. *Supply and Demand.* New York: Harcourt Brace and Co., 1922.

Wedgewood, J. *The Economics of Inheritance.* London: G. Routledge & Sons, 1929.

Robbins, Lionel. *An Essay on the Nature and Significance of Economic Science.* London: Macmillan, 1932. 2nd edn., 1935.

Beveridge, William. *Full Employment in a Free Society.* London: Allen & Unwin, 1944. New York: W. W. Norton, 1945.

Lerner, A. P. "The Concept of Monopoly and the Menace of Monopoly Power," *Review of Economic Studies,* I (1934), 157–175.

Keynes, J. M. *The General Theory of Employment, Interest, and Money.* London: Macmillan, 1936.

Bergson, Abram. "A Reformulation of Certain Aspects of Welfare Economics," *Quarterly Journal of Economics,* LII (1938), 310–334.

Hotelling, H. "The General Welfare in Relation to Problems of Taxation and of Railway and Utility Rates," *Econometrica,* VI (1938), 242–269.

Samuelson, P. A. "Welfare Economics and International Trade," *American Economic Review*, XXVIII (1938), 261–266.

Simons, Henry C. *Personal Income Taxation*. Chicago: University of Chicago Press, 1938.

Haney, Lewis H. *Value and Distribution*. New York: Appleton-Century Crofts, 1939.

Hicks, J. R. "The Foundations of Welfare Economics," *Economic Journal*, XLIX (1939), 696–712.

Kaldor, Nicholas. "Welfare Propositions in Economics," *Economic Journal*, XLIX (1939), 549–552.

Hicks, J. R. "The Valuation of Social Income," *Economica*, VII (1940), 105–124.

Scitovsky, T. "A Note on Welfare Propositions in Economics," *Review of Economic Studies*, IX (1941), 77–88.

Hicks, J. R. *The Social Framework: An Introduction to Economics*. London: Oxford University Press, 1942.

Lange, Oskar. "The Foundations of Welfare Economics," *Econometrica*, X (1942), 215–228.

Reder, M. W. *Studies in the Theory of Welfare Economics*. New York: Columbia University Press, 1942.

Schumpeter, Joseph. *Capitalism, Socialism and Democracy*. London: Allen & Unwin, 1943.

Stigler, G. J. "The New Welfare Economics," *American Economic Review*, XXXIII (1943), 355–359.

Lerner, Abba P. *The Economics of Control*. New York: Macmillan, 1944.

Hicks, John R. *Value and Capital*. 2nd edn. Oxford: The Clarendon Press, 1946.

Radomysler, A. "Welfare Economics and Economic Policy," *Econometrica*, N.S., XIII (1946), 190–304.

Samuelson, Paul Anthony. *Foundations of Economic Analysis*. Cambridge, Mass.: Harvard University Press, 1947. See especially ch. 8 on "Welfare Economies."

Bower, Howard B. *Toward Social Economy*. New York: Rinehart, 1948.

Myint, Hla. *Theories of Welfare Economics*. London: Longmans Green, 1948.

Little, I. M. D. *A Critique of Welfare Economics*. Oxford: The Clarendon Press, 1950. 2nd edn., 1957.

Simons, Henry C. *Federal Tax Reform*. Chicago: University of Chicago Press, 1950.

Hicks, J. R. *The Theory of Wages*. London: Macmillan, 1951.

Baumol, William J. *Welfare Economics and the Theory of the State*. Cambridge, Mass.: Harvard University Press, 1952.

Scitovsky, Tibor. *Welfare and Competition*. London: Allen & Unwin, 1952.

Danhof, Clarence H. Ch. 3, "Economic Values in Cultural Perspective." In *Goals of Economic Life* (pp. 84–117). A. Dudley Ward, ed. New York: Harper & Bros., 1953.

Friedman, Milton J. "Choice, Chance, and the Personal Distribution of Income," *Journal of Political Economy*, LXI (1953), 277–292.

Hutchinson, T. W. *A Review of Economic Doctrines*. Oxford: The Clarendon Press, 1953.

Bergson, Abram. "On the Concept of Social Welfare," *Quarterly Journal of Economics*, LXVIII (1954), 233–252.

Braybrooke, David. "Farewell to the New Welfare Economies," *Review of Economic Studies*, XXIII (1955), 180–193.

Wootton, Barbara. *Social Foundations of Wage Policy*. London: Allen & Unwin, 1955.

Kaldor, Nicholas. "Alternative Theories of Distribution," *Review of Economic Studies*, XXIII (1955–1956), 83–100.

Dorons, Anthony. *An Economic Theory of Democracy*. New York: Harper & Bros., 1957.

Graff, J. *Theoretical Welfare Economics*. Cambridge: Cambridge University Press, 1957.

Boulding, Kenneth. *Principles of Economic Policy.* Englewood Cliffs, N. J.: Prentice-Hall, 1958.

Oliver, Henry M., Jr. "Economic Value Theory as a Policy Guide," *Ethics,* LXVIII (1958), 186–193.

Stigler, George J. "The Goals of Economic Policy," *The Journal of Business,* XXXI (1958), 169–176.

Beveridge, William H. *Full Employment in a Free Society.* London: Allen & Unwin, 1960.

Kaldor, Nicholas. *Essays on Value and Distribution.* London: Duckworth & Co., 1960.

Rothenberg, J. *Measurement of Social Welfare.* Englewood Cliffs, N. J.: Prentice- Hall, 1961.

Fisher, Franklin, and Jerome Rothenberg. "How Income Ought to be Distributed," *Journal of Political Economy,* LXX (1963), 88–93.

Scitovsky, Tibor. *Papers on Welfare and Growth.* London: Allen & Unwin, 1964.

3) GAME THEORY

A very comprehensive bibliography can be found in:

Handy, Rollo, and Paul Kurtz, eds. *A Current Appraisal of the Behavioral Sciences.* Sect. 7, Supplement to *American Behavioral Scientist,* Vol. 7, no. 7 (1964). Ch. 13, "A Game Theory" (pp. 121–125).

Luce, R. Duncan, and Howard Raiffa. *Games and Decisions: Introduction and Critical Survey.* New York: Wiley, 1957.

Some few important items too recent to be listed there are:

Rapoport, Anatol. *Fights, Games, and Debates.* Ann Arbor: University of Michigan Press, 1960.

Schelling, T. C. *The Strategy of Conflict.* Cambridge, Mass.: Harvard University Press, 1960.

4) DECISION THEORY

a) Formal Models (Statistics and Operations Research)

Ackoff, Russell L. "The Development of Operations Research as a Science," *Operations Research,* IV (1956), 265–295.

——, ed. *Progress in Operations Research.* New York: Wiley, 1961.

Arrow, Kenneth J. "Alternative Approaches to the Theory of Choice in Risk-Taking Situations," *Econometrica,* XIX (1951), 404–437.

——. *Social Choice and Individual Values.* New York: Wiley, 1951.

Bates, James. "A Model for the Science of Decision," *Philosophy of Science,* XXI (1954), 326–339.

Bross, Irwin. *Design for Decision.* New York: Macmillan, 1953.

Churchman, C. West. *Prediction and Optimal Decision.* Englewood Cliffs, N. J.: Prentice-Hall, 1961.

Cowles Commission for Research in Economics. *Rational Decision-Making and Economic Behavior.* 19th Annual Report, 1950–1951. Chicago: University of Chicago Press, 1951.

Davidson, Donald, Patrick Suppes, and Sidney Siegel. *Decision-Making: An Experimental Approach.* Stanford: Stanford University Press, 1957.

Girshick, Meyer A. "An Elementary Survey of Statistical Decision Theory," *Review of Educational Research,* XXIV (1954), 448–466.

Handy, Rollo, and Paul Kurtz, eds. *A Current Appraisal of the Behavioral Sciences.* Sect. 7, Supplement to *American Behavioral Scientist,* Vol. 7, no. 7 (1964). Ch. 14, "Decision-Making Theory" (pp. 126–130).

Jeffrey, R. C. *The Logic of Decision.* New York: Wiley, 1965.

Oppenheim, Felix E. "Rational Choice," *Journal of Philosophy,* L (1953), 341–350.

"Preferential Behavior: Decision-Making Theory," *American Behavioral Scientist,* Vol. VII, no. 7 (March 1964).

Sasieni, Maurice, Arthur Jaspur, and Lawrence Friedman. *Operations Research: Methods and Problems.* New York: Wiley, 1959.

Simon, Herbert A. *Models of Man, Social and Rational.* New York: Wiley, 1957. See especially chs. 14–16.

Smith, Nicholas M., Jr., Stanley S. Walters, *et al.* "The Theory of Value and the Science of Decision; A Summary," *Journal of the Operations Research Society of America,* I (1953), 103–113.

Snyder, Richard C., H. W. Bruck, and Burton Sapin. *Decision-Making as an Approach to the Study of International Politics.* Princeton: Princeton University Press, 1954.

——. "A Decision-Making Approach to the Study of Political Phenomena." In *Approaches to the Study of Politics* (pp. 3–38). Roland Young, ed. Evanston: Northwestern University Press, 1958.

Suppes, Patrick. "The Philosophical Relevance of Decision Theory," *Journal of Philosophy,* LVIII (1961), 605–614.

Thrall, Robert M., Clyde H. Coombs, and Robert L. Davis, eds. *Decision Processes.* New York: Wiley, 1954.

Washburne, N. F., ed. *Decisions, Values and Groups.* Vol. II. New York: Pergamon Press, 1962.

Wasserman, Paul. *Bibliography on Decision-Making.* Utica: Cornell University Graduate School of Business and Public Administration, 1957. (Dittoed.)

Willner, Dorothy, ed. *Decisions, Values and Groups.* Vol. I. New York: Pergamon Press, 1960.

b) Empirical Studies

Coombs, Clyde H. "Social Choice and Strength of Preference." In *Decision Processes.* R. M. Thrall, *et al.,* eds. New York: Wiley, 1954.

————, and David C. Beardsley. "On Decision-Making Under Uncertainty." In *Decision Processes*. R. M. Thrall, *et al.*, eds. New York: Wiley, 1954.

Dahl, Robert A. "Hierarchy, Democracy, and Bargaining in Politics and Economics." In *Research Frontiers in Politics and Government, Brookings Lectures, 1955* (pp. 45–69). Washington, D. C.: Brookings Institution.

Edwards, Ward. "The Theory of Decision Making," *Psychological Bulletin*, LI (1954), 380–417.

Raup, R. Bruce. "Choice and Decision in Social Intelligence," *Journal of Social Issues*, VI (1950), 45–49.

Siegel, Sidney. "Level of Aspiration and Decision-Making," *Psychological Review*, LXIV (1957), 253–262.

Simon, Herbert A. *Administrative Behavior: A Study of Decision-Making Processes in Administrative Organization.* 2nd edn. New York: Macmillan, 1957.

5) VALUE THEORY

a) Formal Models

Ackoff, Russell L. "On a Science of Ethics," *Philosophy and Phenomenological Research*, IX (1949), 663–672.

Bohnert, Herbert G. "The Logical Structure of the Utility Concept." In *Decision Processes*, Robert M. Thrall, *et al.*, eds. New York: Wiley, 1954.

Boulding, Kenneth E. "Some Contributions of Economics to the General Theory of Value," *Philosophy of Science*, XXIII (1956), 1–14.

Braithwaite, R. B. "Moral Principles and Inductive Policies," *British Academy Proceedings*, XXXVI (1950), 51–68.

Cerf, Walter. "Value Decisions," *Philosophy of Science*, XVIII (1951), 26–34.

Davidson, Donald, J. C. C. McKinsey, and Patrick Suppes. "Outlines of a Formal Theory of Value," *Philosophy of Science*, XXII (1955), 140–160.

Ducasse, C. J. "The Nature and Function of Theory in Ethics," *Ethics,* LI (1940), 22–37.

Hilliard, Albert L. *The Forms of Value: The Extension of a Hedonistic Axiology.* New York: Columbia University Press, 1950.

Martin, Richard M. *Intension and Decision.* Englewood Cliffs, N.J.: Prentice-Hall, 1963.

Morris, Charles W. "Axiology as the Science of Preferential Behavior." In *Value: A Cooperative Inquiry* (pp. 211–222). Ray Lepley, ed. New York: Columbia University Press, 1949.

Perry, Charner M. "Bases, Arbitrary and Otherwise, for Morality: A Critique Criticized; the Arbitrary as a Basis for Rational Morality," *International Journal of Ethics,* XLIII (1933), 127–166.

——. "Principles of Value and the Problem of Ethics," *Revue internationale de philosophie,* I (1939), 666–683.

Smith, Nicholas M., Jr. "A Calculus for Ethics; A Theory of the Structure of Value," *Behavioral Science,* Vol. I (1956); Parts 1 and 2, pp. 111–142, 186–211.

b) Empirical Studies

Allport, Gordon W., and Philip E. Vernon. *A Study of Values.* Boston: Houghton Mifflin, 1931.

Duffy, Elizabeth. "A Critical Review of Investigations Employing the Allport-Vernon Study of Values and Other Tests of Evaluative Attitudes," *Psychological Bulletin,* XXXVII (1940), 597–612.

Graham, James L. "Some Attitudes Towards Values," *Journal of Social Psychology,* XII (1940), 405–414.

Bruner, Jerome S., and Cecile C. Goodman. "Value and Need as Organizing Factors in Perception," *Journal of Abnormal and Social Psychology,* XLII (1947), 33–44.

Carter, Lanor F., and Kermit Schooler. "Value, Need, and Other Factors in Perception," *Psychological Review*, LVI (1949), 200–207.

Mosteller, Frederick, and P. Nogee. "An Experimental Measurement of Utility," *Journal of Political Economy*, LIX (1951), 371–404.

Precker, Joseph A. "Similarity of Valuings as a Factor in Selection of Peers and Near-Authority Figures," *Journal of Abnormal and Social Psychology*, XLVII (1952), 406–414.

———. "The Automorphic Process in the Attribution of Values," *Journal of Personality*, XXI (1953), 356–363.

Churchman, Charles West. "An Approximate Measure of Value," *Operations Research*, II (1954), 172–187.

6) POLITICAL AND SOCIOLOGICAL THEORY

Sidgwick, Henry. *Elements of Politics.* London: Macmillan, 1890. 2nd edn., 1897.

Hobhouse, L. T. *Elements of Social Justice.* New York: Henry Holt, 1922.

Spengler, J. J. "Sociological Presuppositions in Economic Theory," *Southern Economic Journal*, VII (1940-1941), 131–157.

Carritt, E. F. *Ethical and Political Thinking.* Oxford: The Clarendon Press, 1947.

Lerner, Daniel, and Harold D. Lasswell. *The Policy Sciences.* Stanford: Stanford University Press, 1951.

Dahl, R., and C. Lindblom. *Politics, Economics, and Welfare.* New York: Harper & Bros., 1953. See especially Part III, "Social Processes for Economizing."

Goldschmidt, Walter. "Values and the Field of Comparative Sociology," *American Sociological Review*, XVIII (1953), 287–293.

Harding, D. W. *Social Psychology and Individual Values.* London: Hutchinson's, 1953.

Downs, A. *An Economic Theory of Democracy*. New York: Harper & Bros., 1957.

Oliver, Henry M., Jr. "Economic Value Theory as a Policy Guide," *Ethics*, LXVIII (1958), 186–193.

Parsons, Talcott. *Structure of Social Action*. Glencoe, Ill.: The Free Press, 1961. See chs. 2 and 3.

Buchanan, J. M., and G. Tulloch. *The Calculus of Consent*. Ann Arbor: University of Michigan Press, 1962.

Friedrich, Carl J., ed. *The Public Interest*. Nomos V. New York: Atherton Press, 1962.

Braybrooke, David, and Charles E. Lindblom. *A Strategy of Decision*. New York: The Free Press of Glencoe, 1963.

Dietze, Gottfried. *In Defense of Property*. Chicago: Henry Regnery, 1963.

H. *The Problem of Distributive Justice*

Smart, W. *The Distribution of Income*. London: Macmillan, 1899.

Clark, J. B. *The Distribution of Wealth*. New York: Macmillan, 1899.

Ryan, John A. *A Living Wage: Its Ethical and Economic Aspects*. New York: Macmillan, 1906; 2nd edn., 1920.

Pigou, A. C. *Wealth and Welfare*. London: Macmillan, 1912.

Ely, Richard T. *Property and Contract in Their Relations to the Distribution of Wealth*. New York: Macmillan, 1908.

Carver, Thomas Nixon. *Essays in Social Justice*. Cambridge, Mass.: Harvard University Press, 1915.

Ryan, John A. *Distributive Justice*. New York: Macmillan, 1916. 3rd edn., 1942.

Leacock, S. B. *The Unsolved Riddle of Social Justice*. New York: John Lane Co., 1920.

Hobhouse, L. T. *The Elements of Social Justice*. New York: Henry Holt, 1922.

Merino, Daniel B. *Natural Justice and Private Property*. St. Louis: B. Herder, 1923.

Berle, Adolf A. *The Equitable Distribution of Property*. New York, 1930.

Tawney, R. H. *Equality*. London: Allen & Unwin, 1931. 4th edn., 1952.

Faidherbe, A. J. *La justice distributive*. Paris: Librairie du Recueil Sirey, 1934.

Schrattenholzer, A. *Soziale Gerechtigkeit*. Graz: U. Moser, 1934.

Lamont, W. D. "Justice: Distributive and Collective," *Philosophy*, XVI (1941), 3–18.

Hilton, John. *Rich Man, Poor Man*. London: Allen & Unwin, 1944.

Jenkins, Iredell. "The Analysis of Justice," *Ethics*, LVII (1946), 1–13.

Raphael, David Daiches. "Equality and Equity," *Philosophy*, XXI (1946), 118–132.

Jouvenel, Bertrand de. *The Ethics of Redistribution*. Cambridge: Cambridge University Press, 1951.

Somon, Yves R. *Philosophy of Democratic Government*. Chicago: University of Chicago Press, 1951. See ch. 4 on democratic equality.

Raphael, David Daiches. "Justice and Liberty," *Proceedings of the Aristotelian Society*, LI (1950–1951), 167–196.

Ward, A. D., ed. *Goals of Economic Life*. New York: Harper & Bros., 1953.

Crosland, C. A. R. *The Future of Socialism*. London: Macmillan, 1955, 1957. Abridged U.S. edn., New York: Schocken Books, 1963.

Wootton, Barbara. *Social Foundations of Wage Policy*. London: Allen & Unwin, 1955.

Wollheim, R., and I. Berlin. Symposium: "Equality," *Proceedings of the Aristotelian Society*, LVI (1955–1956), 281–326.

Leys, Wayne. "Justice and Equality," *Ethics,* LXVII (1956), 17–24.

Downs, A. *An Economic Theory of Democracy.* New York: Harper & Bros., 1957.

Galbraith, John K. *The Affluent Society.* New York: Houghton Mifflin, 1958.

Rawls, John. "Justice as Fairness," *Philosophical Review,* LXVII (1958), 164–194.

Benn, S. I., and R. S. Peters. *Social Principles and the Democratic State.* London: Allen & Unwin, 1959.

Findlay, J. N. *Values and Intentions.* Sect. on "The Justice of Distributions and Understandings" (pp. 298–313). London: Allen & Unwin, 1961.

Hospers, John. *Human Conduct.* Ch. 9, "Justice." New York: Harcourt, Brace & World, 1961.

Vlastos, Gregory. "Justice and Equality." In *Social Justice* (pp. 31–72). R. Brandt, ed. Englewood Cliffs, N.J.: Prentice-Hall, 1962.

Perelman, Charles. *The Idea of Justice and the Problem of Argument.* London: Routledge & Kegan Paul, 1963. See especially chs. 1–3.

McCloskey, H. J. "Egalitarianism, Equality and Justice," *Australasian Journal of Philosophy,* XLIV (1966), 50–69.

See also Section G4 above.

Indexes

Index of Names

Subject Index

This Index does not include certain topics for which entries would be too numerous: *justice, distributive justice, utility, principle of utility,* and *utilitarianism.* Guidance to the treatment of these pervasive themes should be sought in the Table of Contents.